The Classroom Formula

Mastering Classroom Management and Empowering Teachers for Success

The Classroom Formula

Mastering Classroom Management and Empowering Teachers for Success

By Ramez Takawy

Defining Moments Press Inc.

Toronto, Ontario

Canada

A Message to the Reader

Dear Reader,

Thank you for purchasing *The Classroom Formula*. It truly was a labor of love and I hope you enjoy reading it as I have enjoyed writing it.

Purchasing this book indicates that you are truly enthusiastic about your occupation as a teacher, and more importantly, passionate about your students' learning, as you clearly want to improve for their sake. And for this I applaud you and offer you all my respect.

As a token of my appreciation and to further help you in your professional goals, I have included a gift for you, which you can access here:

www.theclassroomformula.com/freegift

I would love to hear your feedback after you read the book! Remember that feedback is the best way to learn and improve.

If you would like to follow along with the *Legendary Educator* podcast episodes mentioned, you can access the podcast at www.legendaryeducator.com/podcast and listen to it on all podcast streaming services.

Again, thank you and congratulations on your journey of development and improvement.

Remember to always be passionate, be inspirational, and be legendary.

Yours in Education,

Ramez Takawy
ramez@legendaryeducator.com

Advance Praise

"The Classroom Formula is an excellent reference for new teachers. Mr. Ramez provides concrete suggestions for structuring an inviting classroom space and gives real-world suggestions for developing lessons that connect with students. Keep this close at hand as a reference."

> — Dr. Jennifer Freeland,
> Professor of Education (retired), *Florida Atlantic University*

"This is the book every teacher needs to read before they enter the classroom. It has what you are not taught in your education classes. It is filled with content from experienced educators who want to help you along the way and teach you the lessons they learned the hard way. It is the perfect balance of information, encouragement, and a healthy dose of reality."

> — Dr. Naomi Hall,
> Certified Stress Mechanic, *The Recovering Educator*

"The Classroom Formula is a powerful book when coupled with Mr. Ramez›s story of his education journey. Many who have gone before him have attempted to give formulas that are trendy or niche, often missing the mark of actually helping educators succeed. *The Classroom Formula* is a playbook for success in the classroom that anyone, at any

level, regardless of experience, can pick up and learn from. Drawing from personal experiences in the classroom and supported by expert educators from across the world and profession, Mr. Ramez takes the reader through a full-scale journey of what one should (and should not) do to find success in the classroom."

  — Dr. E. Scott England,
   Assistant Professor of Education Leadership, *University of Maryland Eastern Shore*

"I wish all of my teachers had read this book when I was in school!"

  — Dona Watson,
   Author, Content Creator, Speaker, *Silver Fox Productions*

"Your blunt take combined with firsthand experience is EXACTLY what new teachers need to hear! If they can follow this sage advice, it would go a very long way in preventing them from feeling overwhelmed—thereby preventing them from throwing in the towel."

  — Michelle Ruhe,
   K-5 Literacy Coach, *Coach from the Couch*

"This book is a first-hand account of an educator's experiences from personal fears and struggles when entering the classroom environment to discovering the simple, effective, and adaptive strategies and implementing them to achieve success."

  — Anna Pavan,
   ELA Teacher, *Whitehorn Public School*

"I found *The Classroom Formula* very useful and informative for both new and experienced teachers! It is straightforward and has a lot of useful information. What I liked most was the real experiences you shared as a teacher."

— Isabelle Simon,
School Consultant and former School Principal, *New Generation International Schools*

"I liked that it was real, raw, and reality. The book does not sugarcoat the realities of teaching. As a student in teachers' college, I believe teacher candidates need more relevant and raw stories from which to develop their own pedagogy."

— Isabella Pavan,
University student and Teacher Candidate

For Alexander and Sophia;

The light in my eyes, the breath in my lungs, the love in my heart,

and the reason for my being.

...

To all my students throughout my years in the classroom;

thank you for bringing meaning to my life.

Acknowledgements

I want to thank each person who volunteered their time and effort to guide and support me on my journey in education, from the first person who believed in me, to those who did not rest until this book was complete. Truly, I stand on the shoulder of giants.

First and foremost, Dr. Alaa Aziz—you thought I forgot, didn't you! Dr. Aziz was my trainer at my very first teaching job, before I set foot in a classroom. One day he took me aside and told me "There is something special inside of you. I think you are going to be a great teacher."

Nevine Samy, my former supervisor and my biggest fan. She never stopped rooting for me and would always be hard on me when she thought I was not putting my full effort into what I was doing. She once told me "I totally believe this career is in your DNA."

Isabelle Simon, who has always been a guide, mentor, and source of positive energy for my family and me.

To all the exceptional educators who were guests on the *Legendary Educator* podcast, several of whom are mentioned or contributed to the writing of this book, especially the top contributors Dr. Naomi Hall, Michelle Ruhe, Miriam Burlakovsky, Tammy Vincent, Alissa Crabtree, Dr. E. Scott England, and Mike Anderson.

To everybody who read the drafts and gave their honest feedback.

And especially Dr. Andrew Shipe and Dr. Jennifer Freeland who spent the time reading the drafts word-for-word and picking at everything, forcing me to improve and create the best possible product.

And finally, and obviously, all my students, without whom I would have no purpose in life.

Infinite thanks to each of you!

Contents

CONTENTS

Preface

I was a high school teacher for over a decade and an instructional coach for the latter four years, until the global pandemic forced schools around the world to shut their doors indefinitely in March of 2020. It was then that I decided to temporarily pivot my career path and spend some time in the family business. In the meantime, I created and host the *Legendary Educator* podcast, dedicated to continuous professional development for teachers, where I have fascinating discussions with experienced educators about diverse topics meant to enhance classroom performance and elevate overall student learning outcomes.

Reflecting on my journey, it is important to note that teaching was never part of my original plan, nor did it initially seem like a feasible option for me. The prospect of standing in front of a group of people filled me with profound terror. Nevertheless, with each passing day, I am grateful for the decision to embrace this path.

With no formal training, no background in education, with ADHD and a stutter, I willingly stepped into my nightmare scenario and chose to stand in front of a group of young people. I had to figure it out without any theory, training, or practice. Through my experience, trial and error, research, and effective professional development, and the humbling acknowledgement of numerous unsuccessful lessons, I gradually began to forge my path.

Over time, I successfully deciphered *the classroom formula*. I honed the craft of conducting engaging sessions, fostering genuine learning experiences, and effecting positive transformation in students at risk of academic failure. My journey has been one of perseverance and discovery, and I am compelled to share the insights assembled from this journey.

This book represents the culmination of my experience, presenting a collection of tried-and-tested methodologies and strategies honed over years of practice. Furthermore, it incorporates invaluable insights from esteemed guests featured on the *Legendary Educator* podcast—individuals I fondly refer to as Legendary Educators.

No longer should educators endure the stress that precedes every lesson, the anxiety that creeps up as they enter a classroom, nor the dread that engulfs them as the bell rings to motion students to enter the classroom. By embracing and implementing the strategies outlined within these pages, educators can expect a noticeable improvement in the learning environment. Students will become more attentive, engaged, and focused, fostering a conducive atmosphere where learning flourishes. Let us embark together on this transformational journey toward an enriched educational experience.

Introduction

On a hot Monday morning in August, I walked into school for the first time as a first-year teacher where I was hired to teach middle school English Language Arts. In August, before back-to-school for students, the school hallways and classrooms are eerily quiet; only the murmur and buzz of adults talking and shuffling through the hallways and corridors.

On my third day, after several meetings and professional development sessions, I was called into the principal's office. "Congratulations," he said, grinning in a way where I could not tell whether he was happy for me or thinking "poor fella" in his mind. He continued, "The high school English teacher will not be showing up, so you have been promoted to teach high school!" I froze for a moment, trying to register what was just said to me. I was not sure whether I should be excited or run for my life! Slowly my emotions leaned towards a cautious, nervous excitement, unsure what I was to expect; unsure whether I was prepared to teach high school students!

September quickly rolled around, and it was time for the first day of class for students. This was the day! My very first time entering a real-life classroom with real life students. Oh boy!

Back to my cautious, nervous excitement.

The bell rang for first period and my students scattered into the classroom while I sat at my desk at the front of the class. They were looking at me and I was looking back at them. They were checking me out and whispering to each other about who this new guy was. I could feel beads of sweat forming on my bald, freshly shaven head.

The students took their time to find their seats. The class was noisy with desks and chairs being dragged on the floor and students conversing loudly. I gathered up the courage and finally stood up to start class. We were already seven minutes into the session.

The noise slowly died down and eyes were starting to gaze in my direction. They were getting quiet, but only because they were curious to know who I was and what kind of teacher I would be. I introduced myself by saying my name, "Hello everyone, my name is Mr. Ramez," as my voice cracked. Then I started asking their names. One by one they introduced themselves. Naturally their names went in one ear and out the other; there was no way I was about to memorize thirty names in the span of three minutes.

Then came the time to teach my lesson. I had spent hours preparing notes, creating impressive slide shows, and rehearsing what I would say. I stood at the front of the class next to the board and spoke my rehearsed lines, loudly and proudly. Fifteen minutes into my lesson, while I was speaking loudly and proudly, I started feeling restlessness among the students. Whispers were starting to emerge from the back of the class. Several heads were starting to nod, and eyes started to glaze over. I am pretty sure I even heard a snore coming from somewhere in the back of the class. I commented to those who were chatting and woke up those who were nodding, then continued my lesson, loudly and proudly. But the whispers increased, and the nods turned into naps. Even the eyes that were on me seemed to be looking through me, as if I was not there. At least the class was quiet! The bell rang and the students stormed off. The next session, I repeated my process, loudly and proudly.

During some sessions, I got through the lesson and there was no excessive noise nor exaggerated interruptions, but by the time the bell rang, most of the students were in deep sleep. Other times, I would spend most of the session trying to calm down the class, shushing students, answering random questions, going on ridiculous tangents, or just entirely losing control and end up thinking about my life choices, praying for the bell to ring to end the pain.

I was going through the motions of *teaching*, but were my students *learning*? What was leading my students to lose focus, lose attention, or completely lose interest? This went on for a couple of years until I slowly figured out *the classroom formula*—what I was doing wrong and what I was not doing at all—after which I noticed overall improved behavior, increased engagement, and more learning.

Part 1
Focus on Your Mindset

When I was a history teacher, on the first day of class, I welcomed students who came in with frowns and long faces and I always knew why they were so underwhelmed to greet their new history teacher. It was because they hated history! Because they were used to their former history teachers giving them lists of names, dates, and events that they had to know for Monday's quiz.

When you start teaching, you might be surprised at how quickly the classroom seems to have changed since you were a student. Sometimes these differences will seem overwhelming. Keep in mind that society evolves with time as social conditions change. All social institutions adapt to meet social needs, forming new social standards and social norms.

A BRIEF HISTORY OF EDUCATION

Once upon a time, before modern societies and a modern education system, learning was something quite rare and only available to a select few. Since the Agricultural Revolution in 10,000 BCE (BC), the only people who had access to education were the royals, as in the king and queen and the royal family; the nobles, who were also members of the government and the royal court; religious leaders and scribes who had to read and interpret religious text; and, of course, the teachers who taught them all, and those were few and far between. These were the only people who needed to know how to read and write.

Most people were farmers or artisans and did not need to read and write. Farming and specialized skills were passed down through generations and did not need written records. This was the way for around 11,000 years—from pre-civilization to the Romans and Egyptians, Asian and European Empires, and African and Mesoamerican kingdoms.

Slowly, as global trade and commerce started to increase around 1,000 CE (AD), more jobs were needed for those who were able to read and write. Universities started slowly popping up around Europe in the early 10th century. This was the way for another several hundred years, until another social explosion happened not seen since the Agricultural Revolution of 10,000 BCE.

The Industrial Revolution of the 1700s completely changed the landscape of society, industry, commerce, and of course, education. Suddenly, factories started to appear, and cities were formed. People left their rural farms and went to the city to get a job in the factory, which promised stable pay. New skills had to be learned for employees to work and factories to run. The 9–5 lifestyle was created, and so was the need for formal education.

Formal schools were developed during this time, and they took on the style of a factory. A bell would ring to start the day and ring again to end the day. The traditional school system was born out of the necessity for learning skills required to work in the factory, and so, school itself mirrored factory life. You learn some information, graduate, and head on to the factory to use what you learned.

Unfortunately, some schools, some classrooms, and some teachers still use this old method of teaching! As mentioned earlier, society tends to evolve with social needs. Ironically, the education system seems to evolve the slowest, sometimes even stagnating while everything else races ahead. Desks are still organized in rows and many teachers still lecture mostly useless information. Remnants of days gone by still infiltrate the education system.

What some people do not realize is that we are in the middle of yet another revolution. Some call it the *Internet Revolution*, some call it the *Information Revolution*, others call it the *AI Revolution*—as of the publishing of this book, this revolution does not yet have an official name for the history textbooks. But the internet has changed everything we know about education. Once upon a time, the teacher was the source of all information. Now, information is literally at your fingertips—you can just ask Google, Alexa, Siri, or ChatGPT and they will tell you what you need to know! If you are going into your classroom to lecture about facts and figures, then you are doing your students a great disservice. You must remember that you are no longer the exclusive source of information.

So what now?

A Modern Approach to Teaching

Now you have to pivot! You must shift your approach and change your mindset. Now your task is to teach your students how to learn, how to understand, how to take the information on their phone screens and decipher it, to understand and apply it, to differentiate between factual information and click bait, fact vs. propaganda, truth vs. fiction.

On the first day of class, I frankly said to my students, "Listen, if you ask me who did what when, I would not be able to tell you—and I'm the teacher! I would need to look it up or ask Google. Hey Google, when was the war of 1812?" After I paused for laughter, I told them, "Instead of teaching you who, what, and when, I will be teaching you why and how!" And I would see their eyes light up, as they had never heard anything like this before. I would continue with my intro and say, "You can get your names and dates from Google, but what we are going to learn here is how to look at cause and effect, how to analyze action and reaction, because that is what history is at its core."

This was a different way of looking at history—to them, a brand-new language! I told them, "I do not care much about Columbus sailing the ocean blue in 1492. Instead, I want you to understand why he went there in the first place and what was the outcome of his voyages—the doors that were opened to the new world!" Oh my gosh, now we are getting somewhere! Now we have an epic story!

"Did you know that Europe, Africa, and Asia did not know what a tomato was until after Columbus discovered America?" Now we have origin stories!

"Did you know that, because of Columbus and his crew, and later thousands of Europeans coming to the Americas, millions of people lost their lives and entire civilizations were destroyed? And no, not because the Europeans killed everybody—although they did do a lot of killing—but what killed the vast majority of the native population was a virus!" Wow! Now we have an epic story with a twist! And just like that, history becomes exciting.

"Where have we seen a virus kill millions of people before?" Now history becomes relevant!

As I was going through my history lessons—I also did this in my English classes—I would always end with the same question: "So what?" After quickly going through the who and the what, I would spend a little more time on the why and the how, and always end with "So what?" What is the outcome? What is the effect? What is the reaction?

This is what they should be learning; they should be learning how to learn!

In today's world, students need to learn skills above all—higher order skills necessary for the unknown future. Information and facts are no longer the currency of a teacher—you lost that job to Alexa and Siri! So, you pivot and change direction. What is needed now is an instructor who teaches skills, a coach who trains their students. In today's modern, rapidly evolving world, we will need students who are able to evolve along with society, students who have the skills to think critically, produce new ideas, and face challenges that do not yet exist.

THE TRIANGLE OF TEACHING[1]

What is a Perfect Teacher?

There is no perfect teacher, there is only the continuous striving to become one, as perfection is unattainable. Dr. Jennifer Freeland, retired professor of Education and guest on the *Legendary Educator* podcast, says "perfection is also a false goal." There is only the endless journey of learning and self-improvement.

Different people have different strengths, and this is also true for teachers. The Legendary Educator is not only the ideal that we strive to become, but it is also the collective that is made up of all teachers with their unique perspectives, insights, input, and expertise.

On the *Legendary Educator* podcast, I had an incredibly insightful conversation with Steve Neal, Head of Student Life and IBDP Business teacher, about *The Triangle of Teaching*.

Three characteristics of a good teacher create the Triangle of Teaching, a hypothetical equilateral triangle. It includes being organizational, being relational, and being knowledgeable.

---

1. Contributions by Steve Neal; *Legendary Educator*, Episode 10

In a perfect world, every teacher would be like this equilateral triangle: equally balanced in all three traits. But there is a falseness that comes along with the image of the perfect teacher. The reality is that nobody can be like this triangle; nobody can be perfect. And that is ok! We all have strengths in some areas and challenges in others. Some teachers are incredibly organizational and incredibly relational, but their knowledge level might be their weakest trait. This is especially true for new teachers or for those teaching courses that are new to them. There are other teachers whose knowledge is exemplary, and they have high organizational abilities, but they struggle with forming relationships with their students.

It is important to understand that all teachers have different strengths and different abilities, just like your students, and that is why teachers must be able to grow and learn. This is also what forms a healthy community, where teachers can learn from each other and support one another.

There are no perfect teachers, but there are exceptional people who may have challenges in certain areas. When you embrace that you are not this perfect triangle, you allow for your exceptionalities to flourish.

Knowledge Is Power, but Not in This Case

Because we teach, we realize how much we do not know and we struggle with the idea that we must know everything all the time, which is quite literally impossible. It is ok if you need to spend some extra time prepping for a lesson that you are unfamiliar with or do not remember as well as you used to. If you are confident with what you are delivering at the time of the lesson and the students are reaching their learning objectives, then you are doing an excellent job without having to know the entire curriculum at that point in time.

The ability to pivot and change course if a lesson is not going as you had planned is a critical need for a successful teacher. Pivot if students are losing interest or if questions are being asked to which you do not have an immediate answer. Part of being a teacher is the ability to be flexible and change the delivery of a given lesson. Sometimes, a teacher will be asked to teach a course they have never taught before or a subject with which they do not have much experience. Part of being a teacher is the ability to be able to accept that sometimes you just need to stay one chapter ahead of your students. Have the belief in yourself that you can and will know more than them so that you can effectively deliver your lesson. It may be daunting the first time, but once you get through it, it will not be as challenging the next time.

Try to go back and remember one of the teachers you disliked when you were a student. They might have been a science teacher who was a former medical doctor or an English teacher who had a PhD in English literature; in other words, they were extremely knowledgeable in their field. Then why did you not like them?

Being knowledgeable, although important, is not enough to make you a successful teacher.

Growing up, I had many teachers who were experts in their respective fields: PhDs, authors, researchers—some would say I was lucky to have them as teachers. Tragically, I do not remember a day of their classes, except the days when I was up to no good! My favorite teachers, however, were not necessarily foremost experts in their respective fields. What I remember about them was not what they taught, but how they taught. I remember their passion and their animated presence—not their PhDs.

Being passionate about your topic, even if you do not know all there is to know about it, will get you far with your students. Remember that passion is contagious! You may or may not be an expert in the subject you are teaching, but if you convey passion for the topic to your students, you will transmit this passion to them, and more students will be open to learning and understanding.

The Importance of Being Relational

Students learn best from people they believe care about them. When they believe their teacher cares about them, they will give an immense amount of grace to their teacher. You can go into class and stumble your way through the worst lesson you have ever delivered, and your students will be ok with it because you have developed a relationship with them; they trust you and they know that you care about them. Of course, the next day you would need to go in and redeem yourself, and they will be ok with that too.

According to Mr. Neal, being relational is the most important trait to have because everything else will fall into place. Think of the teachers that you remember. Now try to remember what exactly they tried to teach you. You cannot do it! You will remember your favorite teachers, but it is always more difficult to remember the knowledge they gave you. This is why being able to form relationships with your students is much more important than having expert knowledge. What you remember is the relationship you had with your teacher or the passion that your teacher portrayed in their classroom. You must have the knowledge, this is a prerequisite, but you will not be able to effectively convey this knowledge if there is a lack of connection with your students.

THE THREE PILLARS OF TEACHING

Classroom management is challenging and takes time, effort, and special attention to craft. There are three things of which you must always be mindful when you are a teacher, as important as the content you are teaching. These are your keys to developing effective classroom strategies. The Three Pillars of Teaching are the foundation upon which you build your classroom environment and culture.

Pillar 1: You Are the Captain of Your Classroom

During my teaching journey, I quickly realized something that fascinated me. When I walked down the hallways and peered into classrooms, I noticed that some classes were going smoothly where the students were on-task, while other classes were quite chaotic, where the teacher had lost control and was either yelling or had literally given up and was teaching to themselves in front of the board. Moreover, I noticed that the same group of students were acting differently with different teachers; with some teachers they were extremely well-behaved and on-task, but with other teachers they were doing the opposite, as if they were completely different people! Sometimes I would think to myself, I just had this group last period, and they were great; what happened?

I came to the conclusion that the behavior of the students is not in the hands of the students but in the hands of the teacher. It is the teacher who controls the environment of the classroom; it is the teacher who is the captain of their classroom. A successful teacher is the one who effectively controls the behavior of their students.

Since you are the captain, you need to take responsibility for what goes on inside your classroom. When you realize this and start shifting your mindset, you will start noticing how most teachers will blame their students for misbehaving or for doing poorly in their studies. You need to block this thought; this is a teacher who is not taking responsibility for their own classroom and is blaming the students for their shortcomings. If you start blaming your students for their actions, you give them control and are then forced to go in the direction they take you. However, when you start believing that your class can move in the direction you want it to go, you will quickly be able to learn how to make this happen. When you learn the strategies and have the tools necessary to run your classroom, you take control and can move it in the direction you want it to go.

Do not blame the students. Do not blame the parents. Do not blame the administration. Do not blame social media. Start taking responsibility.

Pillar 2: Be Prepared

To be in control of the classroom is to be prepared and knowledgeable of what goes on. At first you might think that being prepared only means to be knowledgeable of the content you are teaching. While this is undoubtedly true and quite necessary to lead a successful classroom, it is not entirely sufficient.

Being prepared means having the tools and knowledge necessary to be able to implement effective procedures to create a safe learning environment for your students. If you do not have this, the material you are teaching is irrelevant.

Being prepared means knowing your students and their needs to effectively create relevant lessons that will maximize your students' learning. To achieve this, you must get to know your students and learn about their interests, experiences, backgrounds, abilities, and learning styles.

Being prepared means having the ability to adjust and pivot when things do not go as planned. Sometimes the power or the internet will go down, sometimes you will have a fire drill mid-lesson, and sometimes you will realize that you have lost the entire class and must adjust your approach. Have back-up ideas for any surprise scenarios that may happen.

Pillar 3: Focus On the Learning

Can you teach a monkey how to analyze the work of Shakespeare? Absolutely! You can prepare your lessons and materials; you can create a fancy slideshow; you can talk to the monkey about the beauty and essence of Shakespearean literature. You can teach that monkey all day! However, is the monkey actually learning?

It is a similarly futile endeavor if your students are not engaged, interested, or focused. To cultivate a high-quality learning experience, you must set the stage, establish routines, and create a learning environment that fosters engagement and curiosity in your classroom.

In short, you must shift the focus from *Teaching* to *Learning.* When you make that shift, you are no longer focusing on yourself, your notes, your lecture, or your presentation. Instead, you are focusing on the capacity for your students to be able to comprehend and process the information they receive to reach an effective level of learning.

There are several things you must do to establish a suitable learning environment for your students, which we will be discussing in this book.

THE FIVE KEYS OF CLASSROOM MANAGEMENT

Since you are the captain of your classroom and must take responsibility for the actions of your students, you should not blame your students for their negative or disruptive behavior. This also means that what you do—or not do—is usually what leads to negative or disruptive behavior in your classroom. Remember, the same group of students act differently with different teachers, so what are you doing that is leading your students to misbehave in your class?

To be able to take control and create strategies to improve your classroom management, you must first identify what are the causes of negative or disruptive behavior in your students. These are the Five Keys of Classroom Management.

1. Clear Expectations

For clarification, the term "expectations" is synonymous with "classroom rules," but some teachers prefer not to use the term "rules." You are free to choose your personalized terminology.

You may know, in your own head, how you expect your students to behave—but do they know? Are your expectations clear enough that your students do not risk misunderstanding? Let's look at how expectations become clear:

- Outline your expectations from the first day of school and do not assume your students will automatically know how to act. While students are smarter than you think, they are not mind-readers! Punishing your students for acting against your expectations, while they do not even know what your expectations are, is simply ridiculous. Please make sure you have clearly outlined and presented your expectations and that there is no risk of misunderstanding. Repeat as often as you need to until you are certain that everything is crystal clear and there is no excuse for not following your expectations.

- Be consistent about maintaining your expectations. After presenting your expectations, be sure to follow through with them. For example, you expect your students to enter your classroom quickly and quietly and find their seats right away at the beginning of each session. However, a few weeks into the school year, you give up or become too relaxed with this process. You let them come in rowdy and roam your class for several minutes before reluctantly finding their seats. If this happens, your expectation becomes null and void. The following day, if you want to resurrect this rule, you are going to face a lot of push-back because, to the students, this is no longer one of your expectations. They are now confused and unsure of what you want them to do. And do not try to impose consequences because that will not make sense anymore! It is up to you to be consistent with your expectations. Do not forget, do not lapse, and do not make exceptions. This just confuses the students, and your expectations are no longer clear to them—and if this happens, you can go ahead and expect a lot of negative behavior because at this point, they have given up.

2. Strong Relationships with Students

Ask any student, and they will tell you they appreciate the teacher who cares about them and do not appreciate the teacher who goes into class, goes through the motions, and leaves; also known as the "paycheck teacher." Students can tell the difference. You will need to actually talk to your students and get to know them: talk about something outside of the curriculum; ask them questions, let them ask you questions—without getting overly personal of course. Take the time to get to know your students and really, sincerely, take an interest in them.

Teaching hinges on human connection, but there are those who think the idea of getting to know their students is a chore. Unfortunately, these teachers are not in the right profession. Once you have established this link and your students start trusting you, you will see more eyes fixed on you and not wandering from wall to wall.

3. Student Retention

In your teaching journey, you will encounter students who just stop showing up; they stop caring about their education. This is incredibly challenging because if a student reaches this point, it is extremely difficult to bring them back—difficult, but not impossible. There are several reasons that may lead to this:

- The students do not have confidence in themselves; they do not believe that they can achieve and succeed, so they give up.
- The students have unrealistically over-ambitious ideas of becoming something that does not need education: a famous actor, a rockstar, a pro ball player, an entrepreneur, the next Elon Musk, and so forth. And the more they hear about this 0.01% who have dropped out of school and became millionaires, the more they believe they can achieve the same thing.
- The students have joined the wrong crowd and are going down a wrong, and dark path—drug use, illegal activity, gang membership, and things like that.

- The students are rebelling against authority—teachers, their parents, the government, whatever it may be, they are acting out in defiance.

In any case, you will want to catch this as early as possible, and intervention might be needed. You will likely need the assistance of other teachers, administration, and school counselors in addressing these challenges.

4. Student Engagement

As adults, it is difficult to sit still if we are bored or not entertained—now turn that up to one hundred for kids. If your students are bored, they will find something to entertain or distract them—fidgeting, talking to whomever is sitting close to them, blurting out nonsense, getting their phone out, and so forth. What seems like negative behavior is just your students trying to entertain themselves. And I really hope you are not giving them consequences for being bored! Imagine, you are boring them, then punishing them because they are bored! This does not seem fair, does it?

So why are your students not engaged? Several reasons are possible:

- They are bored because you are boring! Are you still wearing the 19th century hat, standing in front of the class and lecturing about everything? Because this does not work anymore. We are working with a highly reduced attention span and if you are not working within these limits, then you are wasting your breath. Your students need to be engaged in order to remain on-task.
- They are bored because the topics do not seem relevant to them. How old are your students? Nothing is relevant to them! They have not seen or experienced enough to start making connections

on their own—this is what you need to do. Everything is relevant if you are able to make a connection. Make sure you are mindful of this when you are planning your lessons.

- Or finally, are they bored because they do not understand?

5. Student Comprehension

If your students do not understand, not only will they be bored, but also frustrated! Rarely will a student admit that they do not understand, especially if you have not built that relationship with them—yes everything is connected! Instead of admitting it, they will act out in frustration. They are saying: "Look at me! Hear me! I am doing this because I do not understand! I am doing this to get your attention, in the hopes that you will see past my blatant disruptive behavior and notice my insecurities! Help me." As I am writing this, several students come to mind; unfortunately, I was not aware of this at the time. If only I could go back in time!

Are you automatically giving them consequences for being seemingly disruptive because they do not understand, or are you taking the time to have a side talk with them to get to the root of their behavior? Are you taking the time to answer their questions or give them a little extra attention to make sure they are on track, or are you going in, giving your lesson, then cartoonishly rushing out of the classroom in a plume of dust and flying papers?

Now that I have listed the five general reasons for negative and disruptive behavior, I want you to ask yourself, can we still blame our students for being disruptive or acting negatively? Sure, these five reasons are a generalization, and sometimes there are exceptions where a student will need particular care or attention for a variety of other reasons, in which case, you have the support of the administration and school counselors.

I know how this sounds, and I am sorry that I am putting the load and responsibility on your lap, but if you take a few steps back and look at the bigger picture, this is really what it boils down to. Are you doing everything necessary for your students to act as you expect them to? Classroom management is not easy—it takes time, effort, and care to reach a level where your students are consistently on track, your classroom has a positive learning environment, and substantial learning is taking place. You are the captain of your ship; you need to steer it in the direction you want it to go!

Focus on Your Classroom

SETTING UP YOUR CLASSROOM

Before your students arrive for the first day of school, you will usually have the responsibility to set up your classroom: seating arrangements, wall decorations, supplies, centers, and so forth. When setting up your classroom, you should always have the students' learning in mind: Pillar 3.

Seating Arrangements

Rows of desks and chairs are very 1800s and are officially out of style. As a matter of fact, rows have never been an efficient seating arrangement for classrooms in the first place. Even back when the traditional style of teaching was mostly teacher-centric and relied heavily on lectures, the students in the front rows were close enough to be in the teacher's orbit and feel connected to their teacher, while the students in the rear were far away, seemingly out of sight, out of mind—and free to do what they wished as the teacher was mostly unaware of their actions.

In a modern, student-centered classroom, there is no place for rows. In a classroom environment based on discussion, reflection, and communication, you need a seating arrangement where the students can see each other and are able to connect with one another, without having their backs to each other. There are many ways you can do this: a large circle of desks, desks put together to form a large conference table, desks in 4s to facilitate group work, desks in 2s to facilitate pair work, or desks in the form of a U or a V.

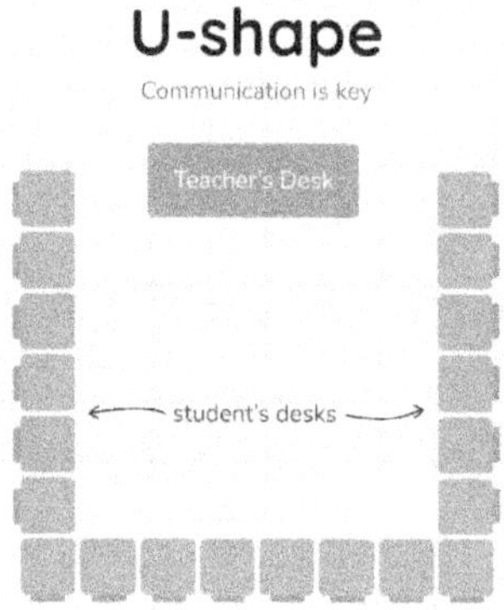

Image: Classroomscreen.com

The arrangement I most often preferred in my class was a U-shaped model: one or two rows on the left, one or two rows on the right, and one or two rows at the center, forming a U. You will need to be creative with the real estate inside your classroom, depending on the number of students you have and the actual size of your class. This arrangement allowed me to see every student, and every student to see me clearly. It also allowed students to see each other, as I quite often enjoyed partaking in classroom discussions where students were able to reflect on their learning, ask their burning questions, and share their ideas and opinions.

Classroom Walls

You and your students spend a great deal of time between four walls. Take advantage of the space on the walls to further engage and facilitate your students' learning. Do not leave your classroom walls empty; not only is this a waste of useful real estate, but also gives you and your students the feeling of claustrophobia, like you are stuck in a jail cell. Decorate your walls with useful resources and eye-friendly visuals.

A "Word Wall," for example, is very useful for younger students who are learning to read, write, and expand their vocabulary. As you teach new words, add them to the wall so their eyes can get used to them.

A world map is always useful if you are teaching social studies. I often went to the map and pointed to relevant regions or countries during my social studies lessons. Not only is this a helpful visual during your lesson, but it also allows the students to continuously browse the map and have it ingrained in their memory—like a subliminal geography lesson.

I also liked to put inspirational quotes and pictures of famous historical figures. I felt this necessary to clean out the students' eyes of all the rubbish and pseudo-celebrities they see on their social media feeds.

As a proud teacher, I loved putting my students' work on my walls. You can have specialized spaces or a bulletin board, like a "Wall of Fame," or put their work wherever you find space. All four walls of my classroom had student work because I allowed my students to get creative and use their artistic abilities to work on their assignments or create their projects. I even kept some projects on the wall for several years because they were so good!

There are plenty of examples of wall designs online and on social media; take advantage of what people have already created.

A word of warning, however. Do not over-saturate your walls with content—this is just as harmful as empty walls. Busy walls are distracting to students and, with too much information, students will not be able to focus on the relevancy of the visuals on your walls.

Classroom Materials[2]

Classrooms need materials to help students learn. The types and number of materials vary from grade level to grade level, and sometimes the materials are offered by the school and sometimes you need to purchase them yourself.

Students, like everyone else, feel good when they have a choice as this gives them a sense of ownership and autonomy. There needs to be an ample supply and variety of materials to choose from, such as paper choice, writing utensils, sensory objects, learning toys, and so forth. For example, if you have a classroom library, you will enhance your students' engagement if you have abundant selections for them to choose from. They need to know that what they are looking for is available. They need to be excited about the choices that are available to them. Moreover, get to know your students and what interests them, and add books that will attract them to read.

However, just like the walls that are overly saturated, you do not want to have too much variety of materials as this may be overwhelming for the students. Going back to the classroom library example, when teachers have every single book they own on the shelves, and especially if there

____
2. Contributions by Michelle Ruhe; _Legendary Educator_, Episode 28

is no efficient categorization system in place—in other words, messy shelves—this will confuse and overwhelm the students who will not be able to choose appropriately.

Too much is just as useless as too little. Make sure that there is a Goldilocks balance—not too much, not too little. You do not have to put everything on the shelves at once, you can change the books or materials over time with the relevancy of the lessons.

Engagement always remains higher when you offer your students plenty of choice and variety, but not too much to overwhelm them.

Classroom Stations[3]

Stations are work areas in the classroom for your students to work independently, in pairs, or in small groups. Stations are set up in a way that meets different learning goals. For example, a reading station is where students go to read independently, and this can be set up with some bookshelves and comfortable seating. Math stations will have all sorts of math activities and learning toys. Likewise for science, art, media, and writing stations, and so forth. Teachers will create their stations based on their curriculum and the needs of the students.

Stations are an incredibly useful teaching tool and should be used appropriately. Be mindful of the materials and resources in each station, as per the previous section about variety and choice. Furthermore, be mindful of the location of each station; some stations need quiet while students work independently, such as the reading station or independent work station, and some stations will allow students to work together, discuss, and maybe even be a little noisy, such as the art station or science

---

3. Contributions by Michelle Ruhe; *Legendary Educator*, Episode 28

experiment station. Make sure to separate the quiet stations from the potentially noisy stations to avoid distractions and disengagement of students who are working independently.

MIND YOUR MOVEMENT[4]

I will just say it: Please do not sit at your desk the entire time! And coming in second place is standing in front of the class the entire time—but at least you are not sitting at your desk! The way you move around in your classroom has an impact on your students' engagement.

You are a person who has feelings, emotions, and may have a bad day every now and then. However, as soon as you enter your class and engage with your students, you must convey an attitude of *smiles and sunshine*; emanate happiness and positive feelings into your classroom and your students will reciprocate with the same positivity.

Passion and excitement are contagious, and if you are sitting at your desk the entire time during your lesson, you are neither conveying passion nor excitement. You are conveying fatigue, boredom, and lack of interest—all of which are also contagious. If you want your students to be excited and engaged about their learning, you must seem excited and engaged, and to do that you should always be moving around and animated.

When you are teaching, walk around the classroom and cover every corner of it. Let your students' eyes follow you as you slowly move around. Not only will this increase the energy level in the classroom but will also give you an indication of who is listening and who is not. If you

____

4. Contributions by Michelle Ruhe; *Legendary Educator*, Episode 28

are sitting at your desk or statically standing at the front, your classroom is devoid of motion, and thus, devoid of energy. Your students may be looking in your direction but could be looking right through you and not focusing on what you are saying.

If the students are working on a task, continue to walk around the classroom and keep an eye on what they are doing. If the students are aware that you are alert and interested in their work, they will have a sense that what they are doing is important and there will be less risk of going off-task. Moreover, as you are walking around and checking their work, you are also inviting them to ask you questions or ask for help. If you are sitting at your desk, this is an indication that you are too busy, not alert, and not interested in what they are doing, so what they are doing is of little importance. This will decrease the chance of them calling you or raising their hand when they are stuck and will increase the chance of disengagement and disruptive behavior. Walking around your classroom allows you to be around and close to your students, giving them the reassurance that they are safe and may call upon you when needed or that they are being watched and should not go off-task—or get their phones out!

When your students are working on a task and you need to speak to one or several of them for feedback or group instruction, do not sit at your desk and call them over. When you remain stationary and call on your students, this causes an interruption to the students' concentration and workflow. If they are unable to resume their workflow, they will become disengaged. Moreover, this sends a message that you do not respect their independent work time nor the task they are working on; their independent time is not important because you are constantly interrupting it.

Instead of calling on your students while you are sitting at your desk, get up and walk over to them. Move around the room, quietly gaze at your students' work, and go over to the student you need to see, either speaking to them at their desks, or gesturing to them to come over to your desk. This will send a message that you respect your students' independent time and tasks by not interrupting them.

You are the rock on which the classroom stands, and your presence is vital to the engagement of your students. Move around the classroom and make your presence known, without being a distraction. Be alert and attentive to your students; be around and available for them to call you for assistance, or to keep an eye out for students who are off task.

MIND YOUR LANGUAGE[5]

Just like your presence, what you say and how you talk to your students is important and should not be overlooked. As a role model, you should always use appropriate and respectful language. What you say affects your students; you will be surprised at what they absorb and repeat.

This also includes the quality of language used in your classroom. Since your students will tend to follow your lead and repeat what you say, try to use formal, academic words with your students as much as you can. These *big* words will inevitably, subliminally end up in their lexicon.

How you speak is also fundamental to the culture you create in your classroom. The way you talk about learning and about your subject—

---

5. Contributions by Mike Anderson; *Legendary Educator*, Episode 44

whether with or without passion—will directly impact your students' engagement and willingness to learn.

Many teachers will claim that they want their students to take ownership over their work and their learning, however, some teachers will use language that is packed with *teacher ownership*. For example, teachers will often say things like "Here are the things you need to do for me in this activity," or simple phrases like "I want you to," "I need you to," "I'm looking for students who can do this," or even "I'm going to give you three choices today." These are all examples of *language of compliance* that puts the ownership on the teacher. You are indicating to the students that they are doing what *you* want, and not necessarily what *they* want or have chosen.

Instead, try to use *language of engagement,* where students are given the ownership over what they are doing and what they are learning by using phrases like: "You are going to have three choices today," or "You are going to get to choose one of these activities." Try to shift from speaking in the first person to speaking in the second person. While this may not always be practical, it is much easier to be *student-centric* with your language when you begin sentences with "you" instead of "I." This will boost your students' engagement because, as we discussed previously, having choice and making their own decisions ultimately feels good, as this gives your students a sense of ownership and autonomy.

SETTING THE TONE

Today is the day you have been waiting for all summer—the first day of school. You set up your classroom furniture, you decorated your walls and doors, and you have all your classroom materials and supplies lined up and ready. It is now time for your students to walk through your door for the first time. What you do next will set the tone for the rest of the school year and is quite possibly the most important thing you do for the entire year.

The Classroom as a Community

Classroom management is usually at the top of most teachers' challenges; we all want one thing: for students to do what they are supposed to when they are supposed to. And no, this is not a *master of puppets* mentality. I want you to look at your classroom as a microcosm of society—a mini community. What are some of the building blocks of any society? In any given society, there are the citizens, the governing body that enforces the law, and of course, the law. In the classroom, the students are the citizens, the teacher represents the government and law enforcement, and the law is the classroom's rules, which I will get to later on.

In any functional society, each member must do their part, so everything flows efficiently, and you have social order. In this case, the teachers must do their part as well as the students. When you have social order in the classroom, you have maximized learning.

When you take a step back and look at the big picture, classroom management is actually a pretty simple formula: it is clear expectations + consistency.

The First Day of School

Let's go back to that moment on the first day of school when your students enter your classroom for the first time. What do you do?

First you must ask yourself, "When my students walk through that door every day after today, how do I expect them to behave? Do I expect them to walk around the classroom, chitchatting for several minutes, taking forever to find their seats and get out their materials? Or do I expect them to find their seats quickly and quietly, with their materials on their desk ready to work?" I assume you probably prefer the latter. If this is your expectation, then you better make sure you let them know.

On the first day of school, you will want to greet your students at your door, and they will probably be excited and hyper, loud and energetic— and although this is not necessarily a bad thing at the appropriate time, you do not want this influx of energy everyday while they enter your classroom.

On the first day of school, I had my students go through an exercise that set the tone for the rest of the year.

When the students enter the classroom abruptly and chaotically, give them clear instructions and calmly say to them "Welcome to my classroom. Before we begin, I need you all to quietly exit the class, and re-enter. This time, I want you to enter quietly, find your desk right away and take a seat, put your phones away, and get out your learning materials." Their reaction will probably be raised eyebrows and a few scattered, "Are you serious?" With a straight face, tell them "I'm very serious." And repeat your instructions again, while you open the door and signal them to exit. They will reluctantly exit your class, then re-enter.

If you are lucky, you will only need to do this once or twice. But sometimes you will have to do it several times until they get it right. Do not give up! Keep telling them to exit your class and re-enter until they get it right. For them, this is a clear message of what you expect them to do every day when they enter your classroom. But this should not only happen on the first day! They might forget on the second or third day—keep this up for the entire week or until you get the results you want.

Clear expectations + consistency.

For the rest of the year, your students will know that when they enter your class, they must enter quickly and quietly, put their phones away, and get their materials out, ready to learn.

Creating Your Classroom Rules

Earlier I mentioned the law as being part of any functional society; the law and social norms are what dictate the actions of the citizens in any society. Similarly, it is up to you to create your classroom culture, and every classroom must have clear classroom rules; you can call them rules, norms, expectations, the law, or anything else that is relevant—"a rose by any other name would smell as sweet." You can get creative with what you want to call your classroom rules, but nonetheless, they must exist.

While a classroom is ultimately a dictatorship, no matter how you look at it, it is always good to occasionally inject some democracy. So, the first activity of the year is to have your students help you create the classroom rules. This is great because your students will not feel like you are imposing your rules on them, but instead, they are following the social norms that they themselves are creating. And trust me, that makes a difference.

So, the first activity of the year is to create your classroom norms. Divide your students into three or four groups—maybe more, maybe less, depending on your class size. Take a few minutes to explain the purpose of the activity: how a society functions, the importance of laws and norms, and the goal of having a functional society, in this case a classroom where everybody feels safe, and everybody gets a fair chance to learn. Then ask them to discuss in their groups and think of some expectations for the class to create a safe learning environment for everyone. Write the question on the board. Give them several minutes to discuss in their groups and to write down their answers.

After they discuss in their groups and write down what they came up with, have one representative from each group read their answers out loud. As they read, write down their answers on a poster board. Hopefully they will mention things like respect, personal space, personal belongings, responsibility, you know, the usual. If you do not get the answers you were hoping for, guide them in the direction you want them to go. When you are done, hang the poster board up in your classroom for the remainder of the year as a reminder to you and your students of the expectations that they came up with themselves. If and when your students do something out of line or break a rule, point to the poster board and remind them, "Hey, you guys came up with this, not me! Please try to follow your own rules."

Just like a society, norms can change over time, and so can your classroom rules; feel free to update your list as the weeks and months go by.

Setting Expectations and Routines[6]

Dr. Andrew Shipe, high school English teacher, recipient of the State Journalism Teacher of the Year Award, and guest on the *Legendary Educator* podcast, explained how he and his students create the classroom rules for the year.

---

6. Contributions by Dr. Andrew Shipe; *Legendary Educator*, Episode 33

Dr. Shipe guides his students to create the classroom expectations by giving them three questions:

1) What will help you learn in the classroom?
2) What will distract you from learning?
3) Do you have any questions?

Make three columns on the board, one for each question, and allow the students to come up with several answers and write them on sticky notes. After an allotted time, have the students put the sticky notes in each appropriate column.

For an experienced teacher, the things the students will come up with will already be in your rules—there are usually very few surprises. The students, however, do not know this, and this exercise gives them a sense of ownership over the classroom culture. This also allows you to have a conversation with your students about what you—as a community—want as an environment and culture in the classroom and will help set the tone for the whole year. It sets the tone both in terms of the expectation that you are there to support their learning, and that an individual does not have the right to interrupt anybody else's learning.

The answers from the first two columns you can take and directly put into the rules—these are the "do's and don'ts" that the students came up with. This is where the students will tell you their expectations of each other, of the class, and of you; some of the things they would like to see or would like to do in your class, and things that they do not want to see that will make them feel uncomfortable, or unable to learn.

Column three contains questions to you; an invitation for the students to ask you anything about the course, the expectations, or even about you. Feel free to answer personal questions that do not make you uncomfortable. These questions allow you to come off as less of a figurehead or an office to them and more of a person, warm and approachable.

Creating Classroom Routines

Instead of discussing the syllabus in class, spending valuable class time explaining each unit, record a video of this explanation and give it as homework: "Watch the 10-minute video and do the online quiz." The next day, go over the quiz and discuss any areas that need explanation. This sets up an important routine for the rest of the year.

This is an effective introductory activity for reviewing the syllabus, but you can also use this method for a chapter, unit, or section in the curriculum, where you do not want to waste class time and focus more on engaging activities. There are things you do not need to do in class and that can be done independently at home, such as watching a video of your lecture instead of you lecturing in person. You are sending a message to your students that you will use class time as efficiently as possible.

After watching the video, the students will take the online quiz that you created for them. The quiz is meant to be a learning tool where they can take it as many times as they need to get a perfect score. The next day, if they still have questions, this can be discussed during the first 10 minutes of class. The rest of the time you can use for activities, discussion, reflection, and other ways to boost and expand their learning. This sets up the routine and procedure for what you will be doing for the rest of the year.

Clear and Consistent Expectations

Setting the tone from day one is crucial to developing a positive and safe learning environment in your classroom. Make sure your expectations are clear and your students know exactly what you expect of them. Remain consistent; in other words, do not break your own rules. For example, if you expect your students to enter quickly and quietly, then this is what they should be doing all the time, every day. If, for some reason, later in the year, things become relaxed and your students forget and come into your class rowdy and chit-chatty, feel free to repeat the "exit and re-enter" exercise with them again as a reminder. If you relax with your expectations and give too much slack or allow your students to break a rule here and there, your expectations become hazy. If you allow your students to break a rule, this sends a confusing message to your students, that you are not serious about your expectations.

Remember that you are the captain of your classroom, and the students look to you for guidance. It is up to you to maintain your expectations and classroom rules, so that the students will follow suit. Do not expect them to behave as you want them to if you keep making exceptions because then they will always expect you to make exceptions and will continue to try to bend the rules. Moreover, your expectations have now become hazy and not clear, so now they do not really know how to act or behave. If you are not taking the rules seriously, do not expect them to take the rules seriously. You are responsible for following the rules as much, or even more than your students.

This should help set the tone and create your positive classroom culture for the rest of the year.

Part 3
Focus on Your Students

As the captain of your classroom, you are responsible for knowing your students, understanding their needs, and forming positive relationships with them so that you have a stable, safe, and healthy learning environment. It is up to you to create a positive culture in your classroom, and this must be built on a foundation of trust and respect.

CREATING A CULTURE OF RESPECT

Trust comes from respect—your students will not trust you if they cannot respect you—and respect is earned. Do not assume your students will automatically trust you just because you are their teacher. I have broken down this strategy into three tips of which you must be aware when you are in the classroom with your students.

Be Authentic

Being authentic means being yourself. Do not act like somebody you are not. Sometimes I see teachers who put on a fake teacher mask: the teacher who is unnaturally formal, overly proper, or artificially professional. This is not you! You should be the same person inside your classroom as you are outside. Do not be afraid to be yourself—be funny, be silly, be sarcastic. When I was a student, my favorite teacher was Theresa Hurley, who had a wickedly dry sense of humor and an endless supply of witty sarcasm. I believe part of my fondness for Miss Hurley was because she was always herself with her students, while maintaining a shroud of mystery around her personal life.

Students are smarter than you think and have an innate ability to see through your mask. They know which teacher is being authentic and which teacher is putting on an act. They know which teacher is being real with them. Students appreciate this and respect the teachers who are real and authentic with them, because being inauthentic is a type of dishonesty. Being real and authentic means being honest with your students, and students appreciate and respect the teacher who is being honest with them.

When you are in the classroom with your students, while you should be aware of boundaries and limits that you set with your students, you should be yourself while setting those limitations. This will cultivate a relationship with your students that is real and based on honesty and respect. When you are yourself with your students, your students will reciprocate and be themselves with you.

Be Firm

I see a lot of teachers who want to win points with their students and want their students to like them, so they are too nice. They give their students whatever they want and do whatever they ask, often going against their expectations and breaking their own rules at the students' desires: for example, eating in class, using their phones, or going to the bathroom seventeen times during a session.

This is the opposite of what you should be doing if you want to earn your students' respect. As I said, students are smarter than you think and will see right through you. They know when you are trying too hard or being too nice because you want them to like you. Not only is this not authentic, but they are going to take full advantage and will ask for everything all the time because they know that you are going to be compliant, i.e., a pushover. This does not build respect between you and your students, and you will lose your seat as the captain of your classroom.

If you want to gain control of your classroom you must be firm with your expectations. If your expectation is for students to put their phones away until the end of the period, then you should never see a phone in a student's hand—no exceptions. If your expectation is that food or gum are not allowed in your class, then you should never see food or students chewing—no exceptions.

This goes back to being authentic—do not make any extra effort or break the rules for your students to like you. Your expectations should be clear and consistent, and you should be firm in implementing them. Do not go against your expectations for any reason, especially not to win points with your students. When you are firm and true to your expectations, they will respect you because they appreciate your authenticity and appreciate that you are being true to your word and true to your expectations.

Be Consistent

Being consistent goes hand-in-hand with being firm. When you are developing a relationship with your students and a positive environment in your classroom, the worst thing to do is to flip flop on your expectations. Your expectations from the beginning of the year are clear and become the law of your micro-community.

If you make exceptions and go against your expectations, what kind of message are you sending to your students? Not only are you not being true to your expectations, but you are also being confusing. Your students will not know what to expect because you do not even seem to know what your expectations are.

For example, to avoid disruption, you expect your students to always put their phones away during your session. Then you make an exception for a couple of students to use their phones if, for example, they finish their work early, although you expect that phones should always be put away. In other words, one day, you are saying "no" to phones in class but the next day you are saying "yes" to phones in class—what will happen the following day? Are phones still not allowed? No one knows! What will you do if you see a student using their phone? If you say "no," then you become the bad guy because you said "yes" yesterday or you said "yes" to the other students.

Be consistent with your expectations. Be consistent with your firmness. Be consistent with what you want your students to do or not do. That is how you build a positive learning environment where the students know your expectations and respect you for having clear expectations and not flip flopping on them every day. If you follow this advice, you will see your students more well behaved in the classroom and will have a better relationship with them and, of course, because of that, more learning will take place in the classroom.

STUDENT DIFFERENCES

Earlier, we discussed the Pillars of Teaching and stated that the second pillar is "Be Prepared." Being prepared is not only relevant to the content you are teaching, but also the students to whom you are teaching. Being prepared means knowing your students and understanding how they learn.

There is an old Arabic saying that roughly translates to, "the fingers on your one hand are not the same," meaning that a ring that will fit one finger will not necessarily fit the others. The same is true for the different students in your class; the lessons that will fit the needs of one student will not necessarily fit the needs of the others. When creating your lessons and teaching your content, it is imperative to be mindful of your students' differences and tailor your plans effectively so that you can reach and teach all your different students. There is no such thing as a bad student, a slow student, or a student who does not get it. All your students are capable—you must know how to reach them. When you reach them, you can teach them!

When planning your lessons, you always need to keep in mind that one size doesn't fit all, and that you need to tailor your lessons to best fit all your different students.

Here are the five basic categories of differences within any typical group of students. Of course, I will be talking in general terms; there are always exceptions—and you need to be mindful of those as well.

Gender Differences

Some schools are girls-only or boys-only, but in general, a typical class will have a mix of boys and girls. On a side note, I will not get into any discussion of gender identity or gender fluidity and will be sticking to the traditional definition of male and female, with apologies to any reader who subscribes to the former.

Many times, in my English Literature class, I would be teaching a work of literature that was more appealing to one gender group or the other, due to the subject matter that was being discussed. For example, my female students were usually more excited when I would teach *Romeo and Juliet* by William Shakespeare, because they thought it was a love story—of course if you are familiar with *Romeo and Juliet*, you will understand their grave disappointment by the end of the unit. Other times, I would teach a work of literature that was set in war time and had violent themes—and you can probably guess which students were more excited about that unit.

Different topics will interest different groups of students: boys and girls—and again, exceptions do exist. But there is nothing wrong with that; you should not water down your selections, so each work of literature appeases both male and female students. However, what you can do is be mindful of the selections you are teaching and be fair in your choices, choosing some topics that will cater to boys, and some that will cater to girls.

But this solution is too simple. Let's level up and see if we can do better!

When teaching any topic, you have an opportunity to focus on several things at the same time; most topics or selections are full of good material and teachable ideas. You just need to find them.

Let's take *Romeo and Juliet* again as an example. If you are not familiar with Shakespeare's *Romeo and Juliet*, you would probably think it is a story about a boy and girl who fall in love but cannot be together, and in the end, because they love each other so much, they decide to kill themselves. Tell that synopsis to a boy and see how he reacts. But at least you have the girls on board!

What else in this story can be highlighted to appeal to your male audience? The works of Shakespeare are full of rich themes, colorful figurative language, and strong plots, but let's look at some simple examples.

There are several great male characters, such as Benvolio, the loyal best friend; Mercutio, one of the coolest male characters of all time; and Tybalt, the cousin who is always up to no good. There are also several fight scenes and comical arguments between characters. When analyzing *Romeo and Juliet*, you realize that it is a story about hate and not so much about love!

With all these factors in mind, you can appeal to your female audience by highlighting the female characters and romantic undertones of the story, but you can also appeal to your male audience by highlighting the male characters and violent themes of the story. Now everyone is on the edge of their seat, either waiting to find out if Romeo and Juliet will end up together, or waiting to find out who will win the next fight!

Socio-Economic Differences

The term *socio-economic* simply means the behavior of people and their financial background. Your students' upbringing and surroundings affect the way they think and the way they learn. Socio-economic factors can be broken down into many sub-categories, but I will list just a few to give you an idea and a starting point. And again, I am illustrating this in general terms—there are always exceptions.

Some students come from wealthy families, while others live in poverty, and some students are even homeless. Are you being mindful of this? Are students able to go home, eat a warm meal, and have enough time to do their homework, play some video games, and go to bed? Or do they have one or two part-time jobs after school so they can care for their family and young siblings?

Some students have both parents, some have one, some have none, and some come from broken homes or divorce. In terms of classroom management, you might have a challenge on your hands for several reasons that I will not get into and will leave it to the psychology experts, but needless to say, these students usually need a little more attention or a boost to their morale and self-confidence.

Some students are immigrants, some are fresh immigrants, and others are still learning English. Are you being mindful of your ESL students? Because they are probably going to be a little slower to absorb the content. Moreover, immigrants usually have a different perspective, due to their differences in culture, upbringing, and worldview. Are you taking that into consideration and including their different perspectives in the conversation?

Some students have lived through a traumatic experience, such as losing a parent, a sibling, or a family member, or being involved in a life-altering accident, or witnessing a traumatic event. The effects of this are drastic. Again, I will not get into the psychology of trauma and will leave that to the experts.

Social-Emotional Differences

Speaking of psychology, there are several psychological and emotional conditions, as well as learning disorders of which you will need to be mindful. Some students have conditions such as ADHD, dyslexia, dysgraphia, dyscalculia, anxiety, depression, or are on the autism spectrum, and so forth. If you are an experienced teacher, you know that every class usually has a handful of students who need some special attention. And if you are a new teacher—now you know! It is worth taking time to do some research or speak to a professional about this, so that you are mindful of potential cases in your class and able to deal with them and give them the necessary tools to succeed.

Learning Styles

Learning styles are the different ways students comprehend and digest information. Your students are made up of visual learners, auditory learners, and kinesthetic learners.

Visual Learners

Visual learners learn better when they see content, such as pictures, videos, maps, graphs, diagrams, etc.

Auditory Learners

Auditory learners are the ones who really soak up what they hear, and they do very well with lectures, audio books, group discussions, and songs—likely the ones that most often listen to podcasts!

Kinesthetic Learners

This group is a little bit challenging because seeing and hearing just does not do it for them. These students need to be physically doing something—hands-on activities were created for them. They need to take notes, ask questions, role play or act something out, create something with their hands, or move around the classroom. This is how they absorb the information.

Multiple Intelligences[7]

Similar to Learning Styles, there is also Howard Gardner's Multiple Intelligence theory—and this is where things get really interesting. These are different ways students learn and acquire information. The tragedy of the traditional school system and formal testing is that they usually only cater to a couple of these intelligences. I will let you figure out which ones.

The original list had six types of intelligence, but today we are up to nine, and the possibility of others that may eventually expand the list.

---

7. Northern Illinois University Center for Innovative Teaching and Learning. (2020). Howard Gardner's theory of multiple intelligences. In *Instructional guide for university faculty and teaching assistants*. Retrieved from https://www.niu.edu/citl/resources/guides/instructional-guide

Logical Intelligence

These students are able to analyze problems logically and solve abstract problems; they are gifted in math and can easily understand and solve math problems. The math teacher's best friend.

Linguistic Intelligence

These students are capable of learning new languages and understanding how to use language to achieve goals. An example of this would be analyzing passages or preparing a speech to deliver in front of a group. The language teacher's best friend.

Spatial Intelligence

These students are able to use visual aids to arrive at a solution. They are good at visualizing and designing. Future architects and engineers. The art teacher's best friend.

Kinesthetic Intelligence

These students are capable of using their entire body and engaging in movement to skillfully address a challenge, such as role playing or demonstrating something. The physical education and drama teacher's best friend.

Interpersonal Intelligence

Also known as a "people person," these students are able to detect and explore the intentions, moods, and desires of others. These are the students who are naturally good with people. The student council supervisor's best friend—also our future salespeople and politicians.

Intrapersonal Intelligence

These students are able to fully understand oneself and to effectively regulate one's own life and emotions. This would be the emotional, often quiet students who really understands themselves and can reflect on their ideas and goals. The psychology teacher's best friend.

Naturalist Intelligence

These students are able to recognize and classify the various plants and environmental species in one's surroundings. This student is a lover of nature and has a natural inclination towards the natural world—the outdoorsy type. The science teacher's best friend.

Existential Intelligence

This is the student who comes up with deep and critical questions about the broader human experience. The philosophy teacher's best friend.

Musical Intelligence

These students are able to produce and analyze pitch, rhythm, and sound. You can ask this student to produce and edit a podcast or write a song showcasing their learnings from a course. The music teacher's best friend.

Back when I was a student, the idea of students learning differently or multiple intelligences was given very little attention, if any; and like I said, evidence of this is still clear in traditional schooling and formal testing. So, students were either smart, or needed to make a little more effort. I was the student who "needed to make a little more effort," and "bright but lacks motivation."

I was never really a numbers guy, nor did I like to read much—but when there was a task, activity, or project that involved music, I always found myself leading and excelling; this was my opportunity to come out from the shadows and really shine. Some of my favorite memories from when I was a student involved music, such as creating a video about jazz music for *The Great Gatsby* for English class, writing a poem about Shakespeare's *Macbeth*, which in my head, was really lyrics to an awesome metal song, or taking a poem and putting music to it to create a song for extra credit, and of course music classes and band rehearsals and recitals. I even taught myself how to play the drums! When I became a teacher and learned more about the Multiple Intelligence Theory, I realized that I had musical intelligence that was never properly harvested when I was a student. But hey, now I have a podcast—so things have come full circle!

Note that students do not have an exclusive intelligence and might qualify for several different levels. For greater clarity, students are usually good at more than just one thing: math and music, language and drama, or science and physical education, so do not feel like you have to have nine different tasks or activities for nine different intelligences. Differentiate your lessons enough so more students will have more chances to be engaged, improving your overall efficacy and learning outcomes.

So, what is the point of all this? The point is that one size doesn't fit all! Lectures, textbooks, and slideshows are insufficient tools to reach maximum learning. A lesson that is not planned properly will only cater to a portion of your class, leaving many students in the dark, and a student who does not understand becomes bored and frustrated, leading to negative or disruptive behavior in the class—remember the Five Keys of Classroom Management!

BEHAVIOR MANAGEMENT[8]

It is often observed that student behavior is getting more challenging. Alissa Crabtree, instructional leadership coach and guest on the *Legendary Educator* podcast, explains that there is a mix of variables that is leading to worsening student behavior.

Social media and hand-held devices have led to a decrease in gray matter in children's brains because of the constant need for instant gratification, as information has become so easily accessible. When things get a little difficult, challenging, or maybe even uninteresting, impulsive behaviors start to manifest. We are noticing a lot of that within the classroom and while misbehavior has always existed, it is becoming more prominent and extreme.

One thing that we also see is that instruction has not necessarily met the needs of our students, where our students are changing, especially due to the COVID pandemic in the early 2020s. The way we consume information—whether children or adults—is very different now. Students are having to *code switch* more often within the classroom and sometimes we are not meeting them where they are within our instruction. To accommodate your instruction to meet the current learning needs, you need to first find out where your students are; you need to experiment with your students to evaluate their current level.

A very useful strategy to manage behavior in your classroom is to first identify the triggers for undesirable behavior.

____

8. Contributions by Alissa Crabtree; *Legendary Educator*, Episode 43

A-B-C of Behavior Management

A is for Anecdote/Antecedent

Observe your students and identify what is happening or the environment that triggers class disruption. Often, the same student(s) will be triggered for the same reason(s). For example, you may notice that certain students become disengaged as soon as you start reading a text. Perhaps disruption happens when you start talking about a particular topic. It can be the tone, the speed, the cadence of the instruction, or the opportunities that they get to converse with one another. It can also be during specific times in your lesson; for example, you may have the full attention of the students at the start of class, but as you go on with your instruction, say, 15 minutes in, or when you start repeating yourself, you notice fidgeting or students occupying themselves with something other than you.

When you can identify that *anecdote,* you can maneuver your instruction to avoid disruptive behavior.

B is for Behavior

When you identify the *anecdote*—the reason that triggers the student— then you need to identify the behavior that follows the trigger. For example, the anecdote is that you go a little too long with instruction or maybe you have not once related your content to your students' lives; the reaction is that your students start to get out their phones.

Behavior like this is an indicator that the students are not engaged in your class. These patterns of behavior are your clues that you need to switch your instruction or come up with a solution that addresses the behaviors; find out how to deliver your content in a way that is more engaging to these students.

C is for Consequence

When you figure out the anecdote and behavior and start working on maneuvering your lessons to try to avoid these behaviors in the future, you still need to develop consequences for these behaviors—disruptive behavior is against your classroom's expectations, after all.

Different teachers have different methods and systems of consequences. Use whatever method you are familiar with or that works for you, as long as your methods are fair, relevant, and consistent.

Something that is very helpful, but not always available, is if your system of consequences is aligned throughout your school. This is especially relevant for high school, as students see several teachers every day. If all the teachers have the same rules and expectations, this will send a stronger message to the students. Try to bring this up at your next PLC[9] meeting.

Having inconsistent systems of consequences creates chaos; some teachers may allow the use of phones in the classrooms while others do not; some teachers may allow snacking in the classroom while others do not. Remember the teachers who are too nice? This is inconsistent and confusing for the students.

Expectations must be set, they must be clear, and your students should be involved in creating and setting them. Along with the classroom rules, the students should also come up with the relevant consequences, giving them responsibility and ownership over their actions and behavior. Once this is established, do not forget to continue to reinforce it and keep reminding them of it, and you yourself must follow through with it, because if you are not consistent, your system becomes brittle and will eventually break.

---

9. Find out more about PLCs: *Legendary Educator*, Episode 19

When you talk about consequences with students, it is essential that they understand the *why*. Even before the undesirable behavior happens, you should explain to the students how the consequence is related to their action. For example, "If you use your phone in class, I will put it in *phone jail,* to avoid future temptation of you using it when you are not supposed to." "If I see you eating, you will miss the lunch break—since you have already eaten and do not need the time to eat again!"

As you present your expectations, also explain the action and reaction, the cause and effect; why the behavior is not welcome in the class. For example, I was always that teacher who never let students go to the bathroom during class time, and my explanation was simple, logical, and clear: "If you leave the classroom, you will probably miss something important and I will have to stop whatever we are doing and explain it to you when you come back, causing disruption and wasted time. So please make sure you go to the bathroom before or after my class." The explanation makes sense and allows the students to understand your intentions behind your expectations.

MINDFULNESS AND STUDENTS' MENTAL HEALTH[10]

Children nowadays seem to be more stressed than in the past. Previous generations, such as Gen X and Millennials, usually suffered the regular pressures of schoolwork, academic expectations, possible homelife drama, and other traditional elements that inflict emotional weight. Today, however, there is the added weight caused by the prominent use of social media that acts as an unfiltered window to the world and all the ugliness it has to offer. Thanks to popular social media platforms such as Facebook, Instagram, X (Twitter), and Tik Tok, your students have

---

10. Contributions by Miriam Burlakovsky; *Legendary Educator,* Episode 36

a front row seat to the tragic spectacle of world affairs. Whether it is scandal, war, violence, or unsuitable adult-related content, children today are exposed to graphic visuals that are not intended for their young eyes and that inevitably cause emotional harm.

Miriam Burlakovsky, mindfulness coach and guest on the *Legendary Educator* podcast, reacts to this present reality and says that although this is an added challenge on teachers' plates, they are still expected to create a psychologically safe environment for their students, and this includes a platform to ask questions, to be curious, and to discuss sensitive, and sometimes controversial, world events.

Mastering Coping Skills

Coping skills are as crucial as literacy and math skills and need to be taught. Coping skills lead to perseverance and a growth mindset that knows how to cope with our own upset feelings. Modeling this as a teacher is very important as it sets the stage for your students to understand that we are imperfect humans and we make mistakes.

Part of the coping strategy is to first recognize the bodily sensations that indicate that you are in fight, flight, freeze, or fawn mode. Once you can identify your physical sensations, you can identify triggers, i.e., what happened before the physical sensations occurred. Next you can reflect on those triggers to figure out how to eliminate or alleviate them, whether by changing the environment or by coping strategies, such as: 4-7-8 breathing, exercise, talking to a trusted friend, or journaling. Everyday practices can also increase stress tolerance and recovery, including meditation practices, gratitude practices, or partaking in a personal stress-releasing activity such as prayer. Other activities can also temporarily distract you from stress, such as: cooking, reading, playing a video game, or taking a walk outside; whatever helps you regulate, makes you happy, and calms you down. However, depressed feelings will fester and you will have to process them eventually. You can do so with a mental health professional, support groups, journaling, and a variety of workshops and workbooks. Every person has their own stress-releasing activity, help your students discover theirs.

Note that to be able to model these practices for your students, you must first be able to master them yourself! Once you can regulate your own feelings and master your own coping skills, you can begin to model these practices for your students. If you need help mastering your own emotions, reach out to an expert to help guide you.

Creating a Safe Environment for Students

There are steps that you can take to create a safe, welcoming culture in your classroom: from the beginning of the year, set up your norms and agreements about mutual respect, about feeling comfortable with discussing difficult situations, about being nonjudgmental to each other and each other's questions or feelings, and being open and curious.

You also need to teach your students how to ask difficult questions or have uncomfortable conversations about world issues. Practice having meetings with your students where they are free to discuss whatever is on their minds: you can include in your daily or weekly classroom routines things like *Morning Meetings* or *Restorative Circles*—a forum for students to come together and speak their minds, guided by you. Let your students choose the topics: it can be something personal that is weighing on them or a large world event and, thanks to the everlasting fountain of social media, there is no shortage of topics to be discussed.

Discussing Sensitive Subjects in the Classroom[11]

While I write this book in early 2024, the War in Gaza, the Ukraine War, and other tragic events are currently raging on in the world. If you are on social media, you have probably seen heart-breaking images and videos from these conflicts. As adults, we sometimes have a hard time making sense of the conflict and the extent of suffering we witness on our screens. Our kids are also on social media and they too are witnesses to the tragedy.

Dr. E. Scott England, assistant professor of education leadership and guest on the *Legendary Educator* podcast, says you have to bring controversial topics and world events into the classroom at an appropriate level; you cannot ignore such topics, since the students are probably already exposed to conversations, situations, or imagery whether from nearby adult conversations or from their social media feeds. If something is happening in your community, country, region, or the world, it is irresponsible and dangerous to pretend like it never happened. If you do not allow for these conversations to happen within your classroom, there is a real danger of these conversations happening outside of your classroom, where they are unmonitored, uncontrolled, and unguided.

Mindfulness Practices

There will be times when the world seems to be on fire and your students are bombarded with negative, tragic, or graphic images due to escalating global conflict, war, or a large-scale tragic event. As the teacher, your students may come to you seeking comfort or reassurance. In these cases, you can choose to hand them off to a counselor or trained professional. However, since your students came to you and put their trust in you, it is

---

11. Contributions by Dr. E. Scott England; *Legendary Educator*, Episode 34

preferable to step up and be there for them if you feel it is within your scope of practice.

There are several simple strategies to help your students get their minds off what is causing them stress and guiding them to feel at peace in their surroundings. You can guide them through a simple mindfulness practice to focus on the present moment and the present reality: "What are you feeling right now? What is happening right now? Are we at war right now? There are no bombs falling in this classroom. No one is hurt. Everyone is safe; your body is safe." Just describing what is happening around them or directing them to feel the points of contact between them and the chair can do wonders for anxiety and catastrophic thinking. Another strategy is sensing into physical sensations, such as focusing on your fingers, one finger at a time. "Pinky finger, ring finger…" without moving them. This redirects their attention. You can count down "5-4-3-2-1" and then redirect to something else.

Sometimes there is a major event that is on the students' minds, large enough to affect the learning for the majority or whole of the class, such as an accident affecting a student or the death of a parent or family member. In this event, continuing with your lesson is futile. You will need to stop whatever you had planned and address the topic that is causing your students' anxiety. An effective practice is to bring your students together in a setting where everyone can speak and listen—like a *Community Circle*—and lead a discussion about the students' feelings. Break the students up into pairs and have them talk about something very specific and dear to their hearts, allowing them to open up about their feelings and listen to each other. Then bring everyone back to the circle and have them reflect on what they talked about. Have students see each other, listen to each other, and thank each other for sharing and showing compassion. These practices make students feel safe and supported.

Resourcing Practices

Another practice is called *Resourcing*—finding something that makes you feel good. Lead the group in a meditative practice by having them imagine themselves in their favorite place. Take them to that place that is their *resource*.

> *Imagine yourself in a field of grass under the stars, in an ocean or in the mountains, wherever you feel safe. What do you smell? What do you see? What do you hear? Imagine the breeze coming through your hair. Imagine the sun on your skin.*

This is how they can get out of that trauma response at the end of a mindfulness practice or group discussion, because you want to end on a high note and be able to transition into learning.

More information about these and other helpful practices are found in the *Legendary Educator* podcast, episode 36 show notes.

AT-RISK STUDENTS[12]

Many teachers go into their classroom and see their students as a name on a class list or a face at a desk, without realizing that each student is a complex formula of feelings, without being mindful that the student may have issues, or conflict at home, or is carrying emotional baggage. Children have a million different things going on in their minds, especially in this day and age with all the technology, media, and torrents of information.

---

12. Contributions by Tammy Vincent; *Legendary Educator*, Episode 17

Sometimes, teachers go into the classroom with their curriculum, lesson plans, and deadlines, putting more emphasis on the tests and scores than on their students as individuals. Sometimes it is a heavy load to carry, but you need to also be mindful of your students as human beings with complex emotions, and hidden chambers of anxiety, fatigue, or trauma.

Tammy Vincent, speaker, author of *Helping Children of Alcoholics and Other At-Risk Students: An Educator's Guide to Identifying and Empowering Disconnected Youth*, and guest on the *Legendary Educator* podcast, says that the first sign of identifying disconnected students is when you look around your class and see students who have an empty, hollow look.

Reasons for Disconnect

To identify disconnected students, we need to first understand the reasons behind their disconnect; and there are plenty! Usually, the main factors relate to poverty, homelessness, addiction, or parental neglect.

According to statistics from the United States, 23% of children under the age of 18 live with their mother only, 3% with their father only, and nearly 4% do not have parents at all, while 2% of children live with their grandparents (without parents) and 1% live with other relatives (without parents)[13]. The statistics shift even more for children from low-income families[14].

---

13. Anderson, L. R., Hemez, P. F., & Kreider, R. M. (2022, February). Living arrangements of children: 2019. census.gov/content/dam/Census/library/publications/2022/demo/p70-174.pdf

14. Juteau, G., Brown, S. L., Manning, W. D., & Westrick-Payne, K. K. (2023). Exploring Family Structure Diversity Among Children in Families with Low Incomes. Child Trends. childtrends.org/publications/exploring-family-structure-diversity-among-children-in-families-with-low-incomes

Remember what we said about socio-economic conditions? There are students who are living through personal crises while their teachers are unaware.

Tammy Vincent struggled as a student, as she came from a home with alcoholic parents and lived through this trauma, and so, is able to relate to these students who are suffering similar fates. She recalled that she regularly used to sleep at her desk in class, while her teachers paid her no attention. If they had asked her why she was sleeping at her desk, she would have told them that this was the only safe place for her to get some sleep.

Signs of Disconnect

Teachers need to learn the signals of when their students are at risk. Students who are emotionally healthy are usually animated and full of energy. In contrast, students who are going through hardships usually have a lack of contact with other students, lack facial cues, and some students may not be able to look you in the eyes. They are not excited, they do not laugh or smile, and they seem to lack the energy and animation of other students. Children are inherently happy and have an innate ability to show off their happiness. However, if the child's emotions become damaged in their early years, it only grows with each passing year, if not properly dealt with.

Sometimes it is challenging to differentiate between a student who has emotional damage from a student who is bored—especially if you have a habit of leading a boring class. To be able to fish out the students who are going through difficult times, you need to make your class more engaging by creating fun activities, even opportunities to just act silly in class. If the students still have a hard time having fun, then you have a sign of disconnect.

How to Approach a Disconnected Student

When you notice signs of disconnect in your students, you will need to approach them. You must first begin by fostering a foundation and culture of trust between you and your students. If your students do not have a sense of trust, they will not open up to you.

How you approach them will depend on the individual student, their grade level, and their capacity or ability to open up. Sometimes you can approach your students directly, but for other students, especially younger ones, this may be a challenge. If you cannot approach them directly, you can implement activities that foster confidence and self-esteem in your students.

Many of these children who are completely disconnected have very little self-esteem and no positive self-identity. They have never been told that they are loved. Mrs. Vincent explains how she helps these students in her classroom, using what she calls the "I Am Wall."

On the first day of school, she would ask her students to write 10 things about themselves. When they complete their list, they would read it over and erase anything that was negative and only keep the positive attributes, then put them on the "I Am Wall." At the start of each day thereafter, she would have all the students stand in front of the "I Am Wall" and simultaneously yell out their words, with a thunderous: I AM BEAUTIFUL, I AM AMAZING, I AM FUNNY, I AM SMART, and so forth.

By speaking and hearing this positive language and positive affirmations daily, the students get to speak and hear positive language that they might not be getting outside of the classroom or in their own homes.

Tragically, Mrs. Vincent recalls students who sometimes cannot think of anything positive to say about themselves, and would ask her: "Mrs. V, what do you think?" Mrs. Vincent would reply, "Well, I think you are very smart." Sometimes you need to be the reason for your students' happiness, confidence, and self-esteem. Sometimes you need to be their role model, as they do not have one at home.

Part 4
Focus on Your Planning

I have many fond memories of when I was a student. I remember in third grade when the teacher put us into groups, and we had to come up with a slogan and jingle for a fictional product we invented; we called it "Inga Dude's Food" because one of the students in our group was named Michael Inga. I remember my fifth-grade presentation about the origins of basketball and how I made a poster and presented it to the class. I remember Culturefest in seventh grade, where we had to represent a country's culture and traditions—and food! I remember writing and reciting a poem in French in ninth grade. I remember my tenth-grade presentation about the weapons used in WWI. I remember a project in eleventh grade, where my group and I made a video for *The Great Gatsby* talking about jazz music, because we were the musicians in the class—and let me tell you, making a video back in the 1990s was not an easy task! I remember presenting about Torture and Human Rights for my high school Politics class. I remember reciting "To be or not to be" on stage for English class. I remember the "egg-drop" in physics class. I remember cutting open a cow's heart in biology class. I remember band recitals, school plays, and the talent show where my band and I got first place. I remember many things.

What do all these memories have in common?

LEADING AN ACTIVE CLASSROOM

What all these memories have in common is that I was *doing* something. In my twelve years of schooling, I can hardly remember a time when I was sitting at my desk and listening to the teacher, but I remember presenting and representing, I remember reciting, I remember producing and creating—I remember *doing*.

One of the Keys of Classroom Management is *Student Engagement*; without it, your students are likely to misbehave or be disruptive possibly because they are bored. I can safely assume that you do not view yourself as a boring person, however, is it possible that you are a boring teacher? Or perhaps, you create boring lessons.

You are a teacher now, but some time ago, you were a student. Think about a time when you were sitting at your desk, looking up at the teacher, and glancing at the clock, wondering why the minute hand was moving so slowly. What are the emotions that come to mind?

I want you to make a mental list of the teachers that you remember; it will probably only be a handful of teachers. Why can you not remember all your teachers? It is probably because you were not engaged in their classrooms. When students are engaged, they are attentive; when they are attentive, they remember; and when they remember, they learn.

So how do you become that memorable teacher?

The simple answer is that your students need to be active and engaged in your classroom. By active, I do not mean jumping around or moving around aimlessly. I mean your students need to be doing something interesting that is related to your lesson's objectives—the key word is *doing.*

Active Learning vs. Passive Learning

To best understand, let us contrast Active Learning and Passive Learning.

When you have a *Passive Learning* environment, your students receive information passively, typically through a lecture. This is passive because the students are not doing anything except listening, maybe reading something off the board, and perhaps, if you are lucky, taking some notes.

In contrast, *Active Learning* is anything that involves the students doing things and thinking about the things they are *doing.*

Edgar Dale's Cone of Experience[15]

Traditional instructional methods have usually relied heavily on verbal transmission of information, most often in the form of lectures. I made this mistake when I was a new teacher, believing that my creative slideshows and lengthy lectures would be sufficient for my students to learn the material. Ironically, according to a study done by the late Edgar Dale, former professor at Ohio State University, listening is one of the

15. Dale, Edgar. *Audio-Visual Methods in Teaching*, 3rd ed., Holt, Rinehart & Winston, New York, 1969

lowest forms of reception of information, as explained in his *Cone of Experience* model, which portrays the efficacy of different methods of transmission of information.

Students only remember 10% of what they read, and 20% of what they hear—a total of a 30% learning rate by lecturing and writing things on the board—maybe giving some pages to read. What about the other 70%?

They remember 30%–50% of what they see or watch, such as a slide show, a video, or a demonstration—but they are still not *doing*; they are still receiving passively.

They remember 75% of what they say themselves, such as memorizing something and reciting it or giving a presentation.

And students remember 90% of what they do, demonstrate, or teach.

Therefore, for a student to remember and digest a lesson, they must actively participate in the lesson.

These numbers are for demonstrative purposes only and do not reflect the reality of Dale's Cone of Experience, as shown above, which does not rely on any rates or numbers[16].

Some teachers will have an activity or project as a must-do, maybe once or twice a semester, just to check it off their list, but that is not the point of activities and projects. The point of hands-on activities and projects, besides being forms of formative assessment, is to engage the students, so they achieve a deeper level of understanding.

I want you to think of your own classroom. Are your students sitting at their desks, looking up at you and trying to keep their eyes open, pretending they are being attentive? During this time, are you finding yourself continuously having to stop some of them from chit chatting, or from being on their phones, or from dozing off, or from doing literally anything else to amuse themselves? Can you blame them? They are bored! They can only listen to you go on for so long, then they change the channel to see what else is on!

Instead, are your students sitting in groups discussing a question, or coming up with solutions, or sitting on the ground creating a model or illustration, or walking around checking each other's work or asking questions? Is there a controlled chaos or a busy buzz in your classroom? This is when you know that your students: (1) are interested; (2) are engaged; and (3) are actually learning!

---

16. https://www.growthengineering.co.uk/what-is-edgar-dales-cone-of-experience/

STRUCTURING LESSON PLANS

When creating a lesson, you must have all your students in mind, with their different interests, different backgrounds, different worldviews, and most importantly, different abilities and different learning styles so that every student in your class has a fair chance to learn.

Again, can you teach a monkey about Shakespearean literature, or about photosynthesis, or the multiplication table? Sure, you can! You can sit the monkey in front of you as you talk, you can show the monkey your fancy slideshows, and even give it a couple of pages to read. The monkey will stare blankly at you, maybe even nod a couple of times as you are talking to it. You can teach that monkey all day long! But is the monkey learning anything? This is where we need to shift our focus: from the *Teaching* to the *Learning*—Pillar 3. Sure, you can teach, and teach and teach, but are your students learning? If they are not learning, then what good is teaching?

While you shift your focus from the *teaching* to the *learning*, let's see how you can design your lessons to achieve the greatest amount of learning.

When you are structuring your lessons, there is always a constant, which is the backbone of your lesson plans: the objectives, standards, or benchmarks of your curriculum. You cannot mess around with those. But it is your responsibility to guide your students to achieve the given objectives and benchmarks, and this is where we need to get creative.

You need to identify three things to focus on while you are designing your lessons: the *content*, the *process*, and the *product*. While the objectives and benchmarks are static, you have the license to play around with everything else to best suit your students' needs.

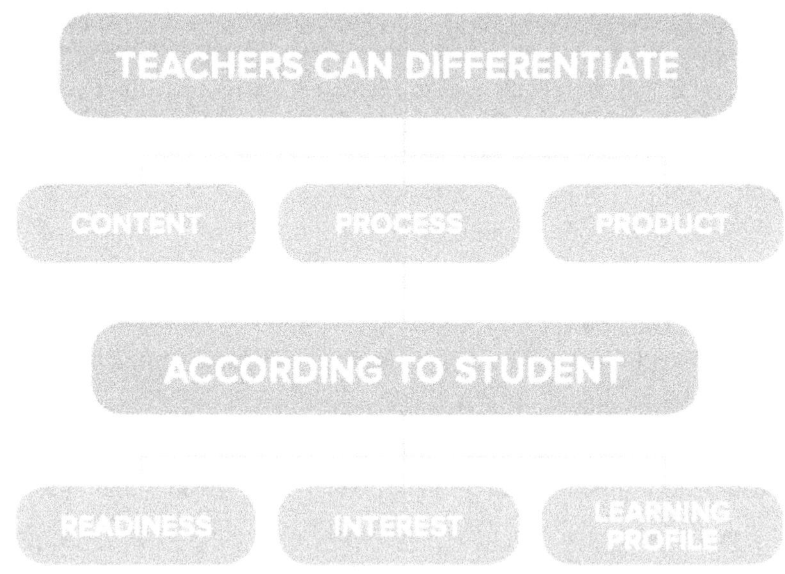

FIGURE 1: DIFFERENTIATED INSTRUCTION GRAPHIC ORGANIZER (TOMLINSON & IMBEAU, 2010)

Image: illuminateed.com

Differentiating the Content

Like what we discussed earlier, you have different students that come from different backgrounds and have all kinds of differences. When you select your content to serve the objectives and benchmarks, you need to be mindful of all your different students and their *learning profiles*. Again, while the benchmarks and objectives are static or constant, it is up to you to be flexible and choose the content accordingly. You can do this by giving your students different content that best suits their levels or interests—of course, while adhering to the benchmarks and the objectives. This could be in the form of different topics, different selections, or different chapters.

When I taught high school Sociology, I experimented with a method that was risky, but that bore successful fruit in the end. At the start of the year, I had my students pair up, look through the table of contents in their textbook, and choose one chapter that interested them the most. They were then required to study the chapter independently, use any resources necessary to understand it, create a presentation following a rubric with several criteria, include an activity and/or an experiment for the rest of the students, and put on the teacher's hat for a day and present it to the class during their scheduled time, after which I would take over, reiterate and review the important points and fill in any gaps that the students may have missed.

The logic behind this was that if the students chose a topic that interested them, they would study it enthusiastically and learn it well enough to teach it to their peers. The act of choosing gave them the autonomy and sense of responsibility over their learning. Moreover, having them teach the lesson would achieve higher levels of remembering and learning, as per Dale's *Cone of Experience*.

You also need to be mindful and flexible about the difficulty levels of what you assign, keeping in mind ESL students and students with fewer skills. But of course, you cannot forget the students on the other end of the scale: go ahead and give them more complex and advanced materials. There is more than one way to meet your course's benchmarks and objectives, so it is up to you to come up with the appropriate content for your students and always try to be flexible.

Differentiating the Process

After coming up with the content that is appropriate for your students, you need to figure out the process which they will use to meet the objectives and benchmarks; and here is when we can take into consideration the different *learning styles*: auditory, visual, and kinesthetic, while also being mindful that students are not exclusively one or the other; they may be a mix of two or more, with varying strengths, or can adapt or use one primary modality for some content and a different modality for something else.

Traditional teaching tells you to give your students a lecture, then give them a few pages to read, and then questions to solve. Here you must ask yourself, is this traditional process of teaching appropriate for all your students? Will every student in your class learn this way?

So, what do you do? You need to get creative! You need to figure out different methods and strategies for students to explore the concepts that will meet their different learning styles.

Visual Learners

These students absorb the content visually. The easiest things to start off with are images, videos, diagrams, demonstrations, etc. Some students can easily digest the content through reading while others cannot. Can you find a YouTube video that explores the same content? Is there a movie or film that discusses the content in a different way?

You can also give them the opportunity to demonstrate their learning visually. When I was a student, before digital media was prominent, students were assigned to create posters that teachers could proudly hang on their wall. But times have changed and so should your approach—although, in all honesty, I used to assign this to my students because I loved hanging their work on my classroom walls! The best wall decoration in your classroom is your students' work.

But let's get creative—how about if you have a handful of different activities for them to choose from? Such as: create a two-to-three-page website, create a short video explanation or demonstration, create a reaction video (like the ones everybody watches on YouTube), create a model or diagram, whether using traditional pencil and paper, or if they can use some sort of advanced graphics program. That sounds pretty advanced, right? Include some complicated options on your list of tasks and see what happens—sometimes your students will surprise you! You do not know what they are capable of until you give them these opportunities. Do not be afraid to experiment.

Auditory Learners

These students need to hear and use their ears to absorb the information; maybe a lecture is appropriate for them. You can also have class discussions or group discussions. Auditory learners are flexible because they also like to watch videos with sound, but can you find a podcast for them to listen to that discusses the topics you are teaching? Are there popular songs that talk about the topic? If your students are younger, you will find children's songs about literally any topic—from math and English to history and geography.

A presentation or oral summary works well with them, whether live in class or recorded, YouTube style. Maybe they can analyze songs to find the parallels of the lesson on their own—or maybe they can write their own song! Again, do not underestimate your students' abilities; if you do not provide the opportunity, you will never know what they are capable of.

Kinesthetic Learners

These are probably your most challenging students. You have to up your game and be extra creative for them because they need to use their hands and bodies and actually be doing something to absorb the content. There are a few things you can do with these students right off the bat: since these students need to get up and move around, they can be your special helpers and the students you call upon for demonstrations. Instead of just reading or listening, they will also have to take notes or summarize. You can have them act something out or come up with a short monologue or skit. Where appropriate, you can have them create something with their hands. When working in groups, they can be the ones who go from group to group to ask questions or check on the other groups' work.

Differentiating the Product

At the end of the unit or chapter, there is always the end result of the students' learning. And unlike the activities that are sometimes quickly done in class, these are more tangible, and often go hand in hand with the dreaded final test—it is basically the test before the test. The end project or product is also a form of assessment, but it is more creative and more fun for the students—and hopefully for you as well—and will enable your students to use their different skills, abilities, and interests to show off their learning, sometimes giving them a better chance of succeeding than by sitting down and writing a traditional test.

Here you will need to keep in mind your students' different types of intelligence, as listed and explained in the previous chapter, because even though not all the types of intelligence are catered to in the formal written assessment, they can shine in the projects.

DIFFERENTIATION IN ACTION

You have all these different students with different skills, abilities, interests, and types of intelligence in your class and you want to give them a project to demonstrate their learning. Do you give all of them the same project with the same tasks? Of course not!

Let's look at some things you can do to help your students achieve a greater learning outcome in your class.

Because this is a project and not just an activity, it should be more challenging and have a larger scope; a more impressive product with several moving parts. And because it has several moving parts, there is an opportunity to have several different tasks that all meet and lead to the same objectives.

Creating Student Groups

The first thing you will want to consider is how you structure your groups, assuming that this is a large enough project that needs to be done in groups. I only sometimes let my students create their own groups or choose their own partners for smaller activities or quick mini projects that do not have a lot of moving parts. But for the major projects, I always chose the groups. And I did this for two reasons: first, they need to learn how to work with everybody, not just their friends. And second, because I wanted to create diverse groups that had students with different interests, skills, abilities, and of course, types of intelligence.

Differentiating Tasks

Because the project has several tasks, the students will work on the tasks most appropriate to them, so when they all work together on the different tasks, they will be working towards producing one main product. For example, the students with *interpersonal intelligence* will become the supervisors of the group, checking up on their group mates and making sure that everybody is on task and getting their work done. The students with *linguistic intelligence* will be the ones who will write the script, speech, or presentation. The students with *spatial intelligence* will come up with the designs, whether video, digital media, or traditional poster or model. The students with *musical intelligence* will come up with the background music, songs, or soundtracks, or edit the audio in the video—or maybe even create a song or jingle as part of the product. And so forth…

Instead of all the students working on the same task, whether they are enjoying it or not, whether they are good at it or not, and whether it is even beneficial for their learning or not, now you have all the students working on tasks that are appropriate to their personalities, interests, learning styles, and types of intelligence. And while they are all doing different things, they are all working towards the same goal and achieving the same objectives and benchmarks. And because every student is doing what they are good at and what they enjoy, you will have some amazing products being submitted to you, sometimes breathtaking and sometimes even surpassing your expectations. This is one of my favorite experiences of being a teacher: being impressed with what my students are able to achieve.

Examples of Projects

Let me give you some examples of projects that I have assigned to my students. Keep in mind that I was a high school English and social studies teacher, but you can take elements or ideas that you find interesting or appropriate and implement them as you see fit.

One of my favorite projects was for the English Literature poetry unit, which enabled them to get a better understanding of the form and style of traditional poetry; specifically, the rhyme and rhythm. After presenting, defining, and explaining poetry, we read and analyzed several poems and they wrote several drafts of their own poems, independently or in pairs. But the final project needed to be bigger—it needed to be epic. I introduced Weird Al Yankovic to my students. Weird Al Yankovic takes popular songs, changes the lyrics in a humorous way, and recreates the song with his own lyrics as a parody of the original. And this is what I assigned to my students. Choose a song you like, print the lyrics, analyze the rhythm and rhyme scheme, then rewrite the lyrics in your own words, following a similar rhythm and rhyme scheme. Then, re-record the song with your new lyrics, in your own voices. Then create a music video. How many tasks is that? They all must agree and select a song. They will analyze and rewrite the lyrics—the students with *linguistic intelligence* will probably take the lead on this task. Then they have to find the backing track and re-record the song—the student with *musical intelligence* will probably take the lead here to make it sound good. Then there is the music video component, which is a project on its own! They have to figure out who will be in the video: sometimes I told them I wanted to see everybody's face in the video, but you do not have to do that. Somebody needs to oversee the filming, somebody needs to oversee the editing and putting the video together, and so forth. Although the assignment sounds simple, it is actually quite complicated and has a lot of moving parts. And because you have all these different types of learners, most of your students will usually find something meaningful to do. In the end they will enjoy the process, and because they are enjoying what they are doing and they are good at it, they will submit something that is high quality—for the most part. Keeping in mind, of course, that they are children—but sometimes they will surprise you!

Another project that I was very proud of I assigned to my grade nine history class. We were ending the unit on Ancient History, and I told them I wanted a newscast about the fall of Rome, in the style of an on-going "breaking news" story. And instead of having different groups create different videos, I had the entire class work on this one project—a very risky endeavor! I had two supervisors working together, one for the script and logistics and one for the video production. One of the students was very talented at creating videos, so he was responsible for putting the video together and had some assistants. And the rest of the students were responsible for doing different portions of the news; I gave them several options and had them choose, based on their interests: there were two main news anchors, several "on the scene" reporters, a couple of people being interviewed, and there were also different segments like the weather, sports, financial news, and even a couple of commercials—all done in the style of Ancient Rome. For this epic project, everybody was doing something they were enjoying, and I was utilizing the skills and talents of my students. Was it professional and perfect? Of course not, the students were thirteen and fourteen at the time! But, for me, it was epic and impressive. Because to be honest, I did not think they would actually pull it off!

I also had several projects in the style of recreating a short story or a scene from a work of literature. Again, they had to organize themselves based on their skills, talents, abilities, and intelligence. Some students wrote the scripts, some acted, and some produced the video.

Were these high-quality productions? Of course, not—actually, most of them were quite hard to watch! But that was not the point. The point was for them to show off what they had learned and have a little fun while doing it, regardless of the quality of the product. But sometimes they did very impressive work! So that was just a bonus treat for me.

There are several examples of student projects on the *Legendary Educator* YouTube channel (@legendaryeducator). Feel free to check them out for ideas or inspiration.

Creating New Ideas[17]

It is impossible to give you a comprehensive list of all the possible ideas for activities: sometimes you will have to get creative, and sometimes you will have to rely on Google. Google is your best friend when you are coming up with activities for your students. Try to look up ideas for activities for any topic, and you will find endless ideas that you can use.

Jonathan Alsheimer, Middle School history teacher, author of *Next Level Teaching*, and guest on the *Legendary Educator* podcast, summarizes his approach in one phrase: "Why can't schools be more like Disneyland?" His goal is to have a fun and engaging classroom, which stems from his drive, passion, and love of teaching and his students.

Mr. Alsheimer takes simple ideas and relates them to his content, creating active lessons in the process. Look at what the kids like to do and what they are interested in and think how you can use this in class. For starters, kids like to play games. Can you marry the games they like to play with the content from your lesson to come up with an engaging activity?

Some teachers are creative and can come up with ideas effortlessly, while others may find this more challenging. You can get ideas from several sources—remember your best friend, Google! You can also collaborate with other teachers in a PLC to come up with ideas. Mr. Alsheimer says, "If you are a good teacher, you are stealing from everybody. You are the best thief in the room. And if you are not stealing from others, what is

17. Contributions by Jonathan Alsheimer; *Legendary Educator*, Episode 31

wrong with you?" There is no need to reinvent the wheel when you are working in a building full of teachers.

One of my favorite projects—the student music videos—was taken from a former colleague and long-time friend Qadir Baqi, high school English teacher. One day, he was showing me his students' work, and the next day, I was assigning it to my own students!

If you have a hard time coming up with ideas, ask your peers. If you have a lot of ideas, share them with your peers.

THE HIDDEN CURRICULUM

There is an ongoing debate about whether teachers should be responsible for teaching life skills to students: some say "yay" while others say "nay" and put the responsibility on the parents. I believe this is an essential part of your job as a teacher. As mentioned earlier, your job of teaching facts and information is pretty close to being obsolete, thanks to Google, Siri, and ChatGPT. You must add more things to your toolbox, things that are relevant to your students' futures, that are required in the current and future job market, and that are essential to your students' overall future success.

Previously, I discussed how every lesson should have a combination of different tasks and activities to meet the many different skills and abilities of your students. This is the perfect foundation for teaching your students the *hidden curriculum*. The hidden curriculum is the set of skills that are not always present in the standard curriculum but are as important, nonetheless. The beauty of activities and projects is that they give plenty of room for practicing different skills.

When students are working in a group, especially if they are working in a group that is not made up of their friends, they are learning how to work with others, especially if they do not always get along. How many times have you been asked to work with someone with whom you do not always get along? Would you decline and tell your boss that you cannot work with this person? Or will you go ahead and make the best of it? You can very much teach this to your students before they face these obstacles in the real world!

As they are working in their groups, they are also learning and practicing other skills, such as how to discuss and communicate, how to agree and respectfully disagree, and how to brainstorm with others. These are crucial skills that they will inevitably need in the workplace.

Another way to train your students on how to disagree respectfully is in the form of a debate. There is always more than one side to any argument and when you have regular debates in your class, this is the perfect grounds to sow the seeds of positive discussion and respectful argument.

You can also have your students peer critique each other before you jump in and assess the work yourself. Teach your students to give positive and constructive feedback to each other on their work, using prompts like "I like what you did *here,* but what if you changed *this?*" or by using the *compliment sandwich.*

If the activity also has a presentation element, this is perfect for practicing public speaking and effective communication skills.

One of my favorite skills to teach was how to identify perspectives. Even though we live in a largely globalized world, there is still plenty of xenophobia and learning how to view, understand, appreciate, and respect different perspectives is crucial if we ever want to extinguish hate and radical thinking. You can have an activity where your students put themselves in the shoes of the other and think from the lens of a different perspective than their own.[18]

One of the very positive things you can do with your students is to teach them how to help their fellow humans; this could be in the form of charitable work or public service and so forth. Your class projects can always have some element of charitable work, for example:

- Your students can volunteer their time at a charitable organization related to a topic they are learning about in class.
- If you teach a topic related to business, you can have a project where the students come up with a business idea and an element of the project is to donate the proceeds to a charity.
- An element of a project can be to clean up a street, a stream, or a neighborhood.

I am certain that if you put on your own charitable hat while you are coming up with your lessons, you can come up with several ideas to implement for your students.

DIFFERENTIATION THROUGH CHOICE[19]

Mike Anderson, an instructional coach, and guest on the *Legendary Educator* podcast, explains that differentiation and differentiated instruction are not synonymous. While you are differentiating the instruction, you must also differentiate the learning. A simple way you can differentiate

18. *Legendary Educator*, Episode 35
19. Contributions by Mike Anderson; *Legendary Educator*, Episode 44

learning without it being an enormous effort on you is to offer students simple choices.

For example, if you are teaching math and working on long-division with your students, you can have a variety of problems that are simpler or more complex. Then you can let your students choose which problems they would like to solve that are the most suitable for their level and will give them the appropriate challenge.

If you are teaching English Literature, you can give your students several titles from the same genre that you are teaching. Instead of having to read a book that is forced upon them, the students are now reading a book they chose because they *want* to read it—if they are interested, they are engaged, and if they are engaged, there is a larger capacity for learning. While your students are reading different titles, you can still implement the benchmarks and objectives, which remain constant. Moreover, classroom discussion will be much more interesting and colorful since your students are coming to the discussion from different angles, since they are reading different texts. Besides, if they like what they are reading, they are more likely to actually do the reading and will be able to participate effectively in the discussion.

Making Appropriate Choices

Before opening this door and giving your students the liberty to choose, you must first train them on how to make appropriate choices. There is always the risk of students choosing questions, problems, or texts that are too easy and not challenging enough, so they can get through it quickly with as little effort as possible to get better marks.

Mr. Anderson suggests that human nature is not about doing what is most simple, but doing what is most interesting. Why would you read a book that is too easy, making the task mundane? Why would you repeatedly solve problems that are too simple, making the task redundant? Students are no different, they want to be challenged, excited, and do things that are engaging to them.

According to Lev Vygotsky's *Zone of Proximal Development*, students learn best when they are presented with challenging tasks that are just beyond their capabilities—not too easy and not too hard. A student may need help or a little boost with a challenging task today but will eventually be able to do it independently. If it is too easy, then they already know how to do it and there is no additional learning. If it is too challenging, they will probably not be able to achieve its solution at all. Scaffolding is needed to guide the student from where they are to where they want to be.[20] Some call this the *Goldilocks Zone*—not too hard, not too simple, just right!

Learning to Make Appropriate Choices

Previously, I mentioned the importance of giving your students *choice*. However, choice is not only about giving your students choices, but about teaching them how to choose well. Your students will not be able to make appropriate choices if they do not know how. It is easy to give your students a list and have them decide which option is best for them, which is the eventual goal, but make sure your students know what they are choosing and can differentiate the choices enough to be able to choose something that is appropriate for them.

---

20. Vygotsky, L. S. (1978). *Mind in society: The development of higher psychological processes.* Cambridge, MA: Harvard University Press.

How can you help your students choose texts or math problems that are in their correct *Goldilocks Zone* and that will give them an appropriate challenge?

Unless you have already trained your students, do not give them lists of choices at the beginning of the year. Instead, walk them through the process. Take time to introduce each choice individually, giving the students a chance to sample and try each one. Continue to layer and scaffold the choices until the students are introduced to all of them.

In the first week, only assign one task that every student must do. In the second week, assign a different task that every student must do. Now they have sampled two different tasks. In the third week, give them a choice between the first and second task—the same tasks they did before, so they have an informed idea of what to choose. In the fourth week, do not give them a choice and introduce a new task. In the fifth week, give them a choice between the three tasks they already did. And so forth.

By the time you are ready to give your students a list of choices, they will have experimented with each one, discovering which ones they preferred and were most appropriate for them, giving them a foundation and the ability to know how to choose.

The Dilemma of Getting Good Grades

If your students' main goal is to get good grades, then this is the first thing you need to remove from your classroom culture. Although grades are necessary forms of data to analyze and evaluate overall student performance on a local, national, and global scale, you do not need to grade everything! If getting the best grades is what your students want, they will naturally be inclined to choose what will grant them this need—

why risk choosing something challenging and getting poor marks? You need to guide your students and put more emphasis on *learning* than on getting good grades.

However, if assignments are not graded, why would your students submit them?

Assessment Strategies

Tasks, activities, and projects are all meant to be *formative assessments*, that is assessment for learning. Unlike *summative assessments* (assessments of learning), formative assessments are casual evaluations to give the teacher information about the progress of their students whereby the teacher can give their students feedback to improve their performance. Hence, the marks the students receive are not meant to be a punishment nor a reward, but a metric by which a teacher will assess and evaluate their students' learning.

Can you assess and evaluate your students' learning without the need for marks or grades?

The short answer is yes, you can, especially if you have created a culture of intrinsic motivation for your students. By giving your students tasks they enjoy, that are on topics that interest them, or that are relatable to their lives, they will want to do them because the reward is in the activity itself and not based on the marks received.

Moreover, if it is an epic project like I previously discussed, you can showcase the final product to their peers, other teachers, or even their parents. Besides enjoying creating the project, your students will make the effort to create the best product to show it off to their audience!

One year, I had the ambitious idea of putting together an *end of year showcase* for my grade nine English Literature class that would be performed live in front of parents, teachers, and school administration. The showcase was a presentation of several units we had worked on throughout the year, and different students were tasked to present or perform different segments: two short plays, five student-written poems, two songs, and a presentation about the results of a charity project we did. The entire event, which consisted of many tasks and countless hours of work and practice, was not graded. Instead of receiving marks, the students had a feeling of accomplishment over the work they did. They were proud to show off their learning to their teachers and parents. The event was executed flawlessly and received standing ovations, thanks to the students' hard work and commitment.

Encouraging Students to Challenge Themselves

Besides grades, there are several ways to encourage your students to take the risk and challenge themselves. As mentioned earlier, there is no real impact on learning if the tasks are too easy. For students to make the effort, they need to be aware of the importance of learning. You need to teach them about the exciting outcome of challenging work and the power of learning that comes from it. They will be motivated by work that is actually motivating and that challenges them enough to lead them to learning.

To do this, you must ensure that you are giving your students motivating work in the first place! Asking them to choose from a list of boring tasks, worksheets, or irrelevant texts—where every choice is a bad choice— will not motivate them. Remember to be mindful of the *learning styles, multiple intelligences*, and overall abilities and interests of your students, making sure you have enough choices and the choices you provide will cater to all your students and their different needs and levels.

Another reason your students may be afraid to take risks is because your classroom culture does not allow room for failure. Sometimes we make mistakes, sometimes we make wrong choices, and that is ok! Your students must have the space to make a bad choice without getting severely penalized. If you are holding up a stick to your students waiting for them to fail, they will never be comfortable enough to take risks and challenge themselves. Let them choose and let them fail. If they do, walk them through the process to see what went wrong and what they can do differently next time, perhaps include an opportunity to revise and resubmit. Perhaps what they chose was too difficult for them and they need to choose something simpler. Perhaps they did not have the skills necessary for this task and they need to be guided to choose something more appropriate for them. Whatever the case may be, do not allow your classroom environment to be a place of fear for your students. Allow them to stumble and pivot without major repercussions.

If you are bored with what you are teaching or how you are presenting it, you cannot expect your students to be excited—boredom is contagious. Excitement is also contagious! Create an atmosphere of excitement in your classroom by implementing interesting tasks and fun activities for your students. Be creative with your lesson and twist what you do to make a simple activity that enhances the engagement process.

If your students are not doing, they are not learning.

MOTIVATING YOUR STUDENTS[21]

One of the challenges I hear most often from teachers is how to engage and motivate their students. When you give your students appropriate and relevant choices of texts, tasks, activities, or projects, and they enjoy and care about what they are working on, not only will they be motivated to learn and to create, but they will put their heart and soul into it. The goal is to have engaged and self-motivated students.

These are the six motivators that will get your students interested in learning, doing the work, and challenging themselves.

1. **Autonomy:** If your students do not have the ability to choose, if they do not have any power or control over what they do or how they do it, they will not have sufficient motivation to complete the task to its fullest potential. Let them choose, let them decide, let them have ownership over their learning.

2. **Competence:** It is difficult to be motivated if one believes that improvement is hopeless. If your students do not believe they are good at something or if they do not see hope in learning or improving, they will not be motivated to learn. Your students must be aware of a clear path you have paved of their learning direction and ultimate goals, which includes the steps they need to take to get there.

3. **Purpose:** Your students need to know why they are doing what you assigned or why they are learning what you are presenting. Moreover, the purpose must matter to the students. "Someday you are going to need it" is not a sufficient explanation for the purpose of the lesson or activity.

---

21. Contributions by Mike Anderson; *Legendary Educator*, Episode 44

4. **Belonging:** Your students need to feel like they belong to the learning community that you have created. Their decisions matter; their opinions matter; their input matters; their feelings matter. Their voices are heard in the classroom, and they are part of the conversation. Invite every student to engage in pair work and group discussions, where they feel connected with other students and with you.

5. **Curiosity:** Kids are naturally curious. Take advantage of this and use their curiosity to foster engagement by tapping into what they like and what they are curious about.

6. **Fun:** When kids are having fun, they are engaged, and when they are engaged, they are learning. If your students are going into your classroom knowing and expecting that they are going to have fun, you will have a room full of motivated students, ready to learn.[22]

---

22. Anderson, Mike. *Tackling the motivation crisis: How to activate student learning without behavior charts, pizza parties, or other hard-to-quit incentive systems.* ASCD, 2021.

Part 5
Focus on Your Health[23]

Teaching is a difficult and stressful job. It is not a secret that teachers are overwhelmed, overworked, and carry a lot on their plates. At the end of each school day, you are tired, your head hurts, your throat hurts from talking all day, your feet hurt from standing all day; everything hurts. You have a group of humans in your class for which you are responsible and must remain vigilant at all times to keep them safe while you are in the process of teaching them. You are constantly focusing on the curriculum, standards, and deadlines. Moreover, the administration is always asking for more and parents are never happy. It is quite a load to carry.

Teachers are usually solely represented by their title, often forgotten as whole people with complex emotions, just like students, as mentioned earlier. There is much more to a teacher than just being a teacher! Your stress is cumulative: you worry about your home, you worry about your family, you worry about your finances, you worry about your health, you worry about your future, and so forth.

---

23. Contributions by Dr. Naomi Hall; *Legendary Educator*, Episode 29

Unfortunately, the stress that originates in your classroom may sneak its way into your personal life, affecting your health, your relationships, your marriage or homelife, your productivity, sometimes even leading many teachers to quit the job that they love—essentially, burning out.

Dr. Naomi Hall is a repeat guest on the *Legendary Educator* podcast; she is a stress management coach and founder of The Recovering Educator, a service that helps teachers overcome stress and guides them to lead healthier lives. She explains that we must work on our mindset: be mindful of how we handle the things that come at us, how we think and what we feed our minds, so that we are a whole person ready to take on the stress that comes at us in the classroom, in the hallways, from administration, or from parents. A calm and clear mind helps teachers handle what comes at them each day.

Stress and burnout are the leading causes of career change and early retirement for teachers. This is an unfortunate fact. However, Dr. Hall explains that with some routine changes and positive actions, it is possible to conquer stress and have a healthy mind that can take on any challenge. The catch is, Dr. Hall explains, that these need to be turned into habits.

FIVE HABITS FOR STAYING HEALTHY DURING THE SCHOOL YEAR

1. Give Yourself Grace

We are our own worst critics. Many educators take things personally and beat themselves up over every little thing. There will be rough days. There will be those emails from parents, critics, or your boss. You need to stop beating yourself up and give yourself grace. Just breathe in and breathe out. It is going to be alright. You will make mistakes, and that is ok.

Just as you teach your students that they learn most through failure, you should also be confident in your mistakes; let your students know that you have messed up: "I messed up, please forgive me." "I messed up and I will learn from this experience." "I messed up and I will move forward despite my mistakes."

No one expects you to be perfect. When things are not working the way you want them to, they are not moving as smoothly as you want them to, your students are not as well behaved as you want them to be, your classroom management is not as on point as you want it to be, just take a breath and give yourself grace. Even the most experienced teachers have their off days, and so will you. Just breathe in and breathe out. It is going to be alright.

2. Ditch the Negativity

Negativity is everywhere; it is all around us. It is coming at you from all directions. You must learn to ditch the negativity.

Look at the people surrounding you. Are you surrounding yourself with people who are constantly venting and negative? You might need to change that. You might need to avoid the teachers' rooms. This can be difficult because your colleagues and support system are usually found there, but sometimes you need to close the door and have lunch by yourself because the negativity will draw you down. Find the teachers who will build you up, encourage you, and help you move forward in a positive direction. Problem finders are everywhere; you want to surround yourself with problem solvers.

In a study out of Ohio State University "researchers found that when people wrote down their thoughts on a piece of paper and then threw the paper away, they mentally discarded the thoughts as well."[24] These people were able to move forward in a more positive direction than people who just noticed their thoughts or did not do anything to stop them. "The results of a 2020 study suggest that people typically have more than 6,000 thoughts per day," and while some thoughts are positive while others negative, "unpleasant thoughts might have a lingering impact on your mood and state of mind."[25] Learn to notice the conversation that is going on in your head. Scribble down those negative thoughts, crumble them up, throw them away and move forward.

Turn off your social media, turn off the news, turn off any source of negativity and move forward in a positive direction. You can substitute this by reading a book or partaking in your favorite hobby, going for a walk, or doing something that brings you joy and relaxes your mind. As the saying goes, if it bleeds, it leads, and there is hardly anything in the news or on social media that does not bleed. You can curate your social media to see more of what you want to see (positive things) and see less of what or who you do not want to see (negative things).

---

24. Grabmeier, J. Bothered by Negative, Unwanted Thoughts? Just Throw Them Away. *Ohio State News*. November 25, 2012, from https://news.osu.edu/bothered-by-nega-tive-unwanted-thoughts-just-throw-them-away/

25. Raypole, Crystal. How Many Thoughts Do You Have Each Day? And Other Things to Think About. *Healthline*. February 8, 2022. From https://www.healthline.com/health/how-many-thoughts-per-day

3. Move Your Body

Many people often make excuses, like "I don't have time," to avoid exercising. We need to change this mindset: exercise is crucial! Movement is medicine for your body and for your mind. If you are going to manage your stress well, you must move your body. Even a few minutes of exercise makes a difference. You do not have to go to the gym. You can do something you love and enjoy and can do at or around your home, such as taking a walk, bicycling, yoga, or swimming if you have a pool. You can start out small with 5 minutes of movement, making 30 minutes your goal. These 30 minutes that you dedicate to moving your body are going to give you about an hour a day of increased energy, focus and productivity. Find something that you enjoy doing and move your body.

4. Fuel and Hydrate Your Body

When you are dehydrated, your brain does not function at its best. Finding time to go to the bathroom is a daily challenge for teachers, but nevertheless, you must continuously hydrate. Start the day with eight ounces of water, since you are waking up dehydrated, and continue during the day. Use electrolytes to make hydration more effective.

Coffee and sugar are not effective fuels and liquids for your body. The popular stereotype is that teachers run on coffee and sugar, but this is a very unhealthy choice. You need to put good fuel into your body. Make sure that you are getting enough protein and vegetables. There are easy ways to get protein in your lunch at work. You are usually eating while you are planning, prepping, copying, or meeting with students, so include some healthy snacks that are easy to pack and that you can eat on the go: baby carrots, yogurt, cheese sticks, and so forth.

Start by building small habits to get yourself moving in the right direction. Start with eight ounces of water first thing in the morning. Include some healthy snacks in your lunch, then try to be more creative with your healthy lunch choices. Plan and prepare your lunch ahead of time. Find healthy foods that you enjoy that will fuel your body.

Make sure you include vegetables, protein, and good, fiber-filled carbs. Look for whole wheat and whole grain types of foods. Look for carbs and protein that are not processed. Make small, gradual swaps. For example, instead of having a muffin for breakfast, have oatmeal and yogurt. Instead of getting coffee from your favorite coffee shop and putting too much sugar, make coffee at home and cut out some of those sugars.

Protein is going to help level your blood sugar. Focus on simple whole nutrition and good hydration. These are going to keep you level, balanced, and will help you think more clearly and perform better.

5. Sleep

The most important thing when it comes to stress management recovery performance is sleep. The studies are clear on the need to sleep seven to nine hours per day. When you get more sleep, you will be more effective, you will have more clarity, you will have more energy, you will perform better, and you will improve your immunity.

By planning your day properly and using the hours in the day efficiently, you will be able to schedule sufficient sleep time. Do not be the victim of: "I just don't have time!" "I have too much to do to go to bed early." "I'll sleep when I'm dead."

So how can you get more sleep?

Set yourself up for a good sleep with a good nighttime routine that will enable you to get enough sleep so you do not feel stress and anxiety first thing in the morning.

Nighttime Routine 3-2-1

- **3 hours before bed:** Stop eating so that your body can digest and start getting into its state of *rest and digest*.
- **2 hours before bed:** Stop working so that your brain can begin to relax and get ready for sleep.
- **1 hour before bed:** Stop using all screens so that your brain can wind down and start to create melatonin, a hormone that regulates sleep.

Make sure your lunch and breakfast are all set, and your bag is packed, and clothes are set out for the next day, so you are not running around trying to find everything in the morning. If everything is prepared from the night before, you will not wake up having to worry about tasks first thing in the morning.

Do some restful activities leading up to bed. You can try some journaling or some breathing exercises. You might try some gentle yoga, stretching, or a warm shower—or a cold shower, depending on your preference. You can have a warm cup of decaffeinated or herbal tea while you read something you enjoy—read an actual book, no screens! Do an activity that will cause your body and mind to start to slow down. If you go from task to task and your mind is constantly busy, then you abruptly jump into bed to sleep, your mind and your body will still be going at that speed, and they will not be ready for sleep; you are going to lay there staring at the ceiling for a long time. When you have a routine that prepares your mind and body for sleep, you will fall asleep faster, sleep better, and sleep for longer.

If you are currently not getting enough sleep, start making gradual changes; add an extra two minutes of sleep each night. Gradually increase the amount of sleep that you are getting until you find yourself waking up rested. If you are oversleeping on weekends or days off, this usually means that you are not getting enough sleep during the week. If you are waking up groggy or struggling to get out of bed, then you are not getting enough sleep during the week. When you get enough sleep, you will struggle less with anxiety, depression, and mood swings. Getting the proper amount of sleep improves energy levels, helps clear the mind, improves focus and will put you in a better mood.

DEVELOPING HABITS

These five tips sound simple but they are not always easy to implement, especially if you do not have routines in place. Dr. Hall encourages us to keep it simple. Create yourself a habit wish-list of things you want as habits related to movement, nutrition, hydration, and sleep, as well as giving yourself grace and ditching the negativity. But we can only develop one habit at a time, so choose one habit to work on each month. There are ten months in the school year, so you can work on one habit every month. Give yourself a 30-day challenge every month from September to June. Maybe September is 30 days of movement. Maybe October is 30 days of getting your full, daily hydration. Create your own 30-day challenges and grab a friend and get them to do it with you.

If you can get a positive mindset, good movement, nutrition, hydration, and good sleep, you will be in a healthier place to manage stress. Remember that we cannot get rid of stress, we can only manage it. We cannot change the entire education system, but we can work on ourselves and control the controllable, so we are in a better place to face the stress and the challenges that come at us every day.

Conclusion
Final Thoughts

If you made it this far into the book, you are probably feeling very overwhelmed by the amount of information that was presented to you—all the things you need to consider and plan for. But fear not, no one expects you to be perfect, and neither should you! We all try to do our best by learning and preparing as much as possible, however, you must accept that perfection is unattainable. There were times when I had ineffective lessons and there were times when I failed to reach a student. It is an unfortunate part of our job; just like doctors cannot save every patient, teachers cannot teach every student.

My guide and mentor, and guest on the *Legendary Educator* podcast, Dr. Jennifer Freeland, retired professor of Educational Leadership always says "How do you eat an elephant? One bite at a time!" Do not overwhelm yourself by attempting to swallow the entire elephant and implement everything at once. Take it one step at a time.

Before you go into your classroom, work on your mindset. Then, during the first couple of days of school, set up your classroom and implement the strategies and routines for setting up your classroom culture. Then you have the whole year to work on figuring out how to implement effective lesson plans and activities. Add something new every lesson; implement a new idea every unit; start a new routine every quarter or semester. Remember, slow and steady wins the race; do not attempt to implement the entire book from the first day of school!

OVERVIEW OF A SUCCESSFUL TEACHER[26]

One of my mentors, Isabelle Simon, School Principal and my first guest on the *Legendary Educator* podcast, painted a picture of a successful teacher, which she formed from her vast experience in education.

A successful teacher is always loving. They are always well prepared. They know their subject well and in-depth. They must be able to deliver their content to all types of learners. They must include engaging hands-on activities in their lessons. Their objectives are clear, and the learning outcome is clear. They are lifelong learners who continuously read, research, and learn to be able to constantly adapt to change. Most importantly, they have to set the tone from day one.

There is no such thing as a perfect teacher. Teachers will make mistakes and reflect every day to further improve. Reflection is a key part of your daily routine as a teacher; reflect at the beginning of the lesson, during the lesson, and when the lesson has ended, and see where you can improve.

---

26. Contributions by Isabelle Simon; *Legendary Educator*, Episode 2

WHY SOME TEACHERS QUIT

From her 40 years of experience in education, Mrs. Simon came to a conclusion about some of the reasons why teachers quit and pursue other careers.

Many teachers quit prematurely because they do not have the patience and perseverance to continue. They quit too soon, before acquiring the necessary skills to be an effective teacher; they do not give themselves a chance. Nobody goes into the classroom the first time fully experienced and knowing what to do; this takes time, effort, and experience.

This usually stems from their poor classroom management skills, which they have not yet tuned and perfected. They complain about the students, that they are too noisy and do not listen. There are ways to improve your classroom management skills, whether by visiting the classroom of more experienced teachers, reading books, or taking courses and PDs. Classroom management is the most important skill; if you cannot manage your class, no learning is taking place.

A FINAL NOTE

You became a teacher not for the riches and the fame. You became a teacher because you are passionate about learning and about your students succeeding and prospering. You are passionate about building a bright future by creating competent and capable citizens of society. Do not forget this and do not let the flame of passion inside you extinguish. Teaching is challenging but is truly the most rewarding job.

If you are a new teacher, take the knowledge you have gained from this book and use it efficiently; you will hit the ground running and be ahead of the game. But remember, it takes time to create your routines and find your stride. Give yourself a chance and do not give up.

If you are an experienced teacher but are still facing challenges, do not give up! I applaud you for taking steps to improve your performance, like reading this book. This means that the passion inside you is still alive! Keep going, keep learning, and keep improving.

Advice for New Teachers from Expert Educators

On the *Legendary Educator* podcast, experienced teachers were asked to give their advice to new teachers going into the classroom for the first time.

Isabelle Simon[27]

School Principal and Consultant, New Generation International Schools

Set the tone from day one! Kids are very smart. They know how to test you. They know who to listen to and they know who they will be driving up the wall. Do not underestimate their intelligence.

Alissa Crabtree[28]

Instructional Coach, Crabtree Coaching

First, I am going to give them a big hug and just be like, welcome to the best profession in the world! I know that there are so many negative

---

27. *Legendary Educator*, Episode 2

28. *Legendary Educator*, Episode 44

things out there about education. But let me tell you, it is so rewarding, especially if you are someone who wants to make an impact in the world. You are in a great position to do that.

I live in Houston, Texas and one of my favorite things is when my former students drive through Houston and call me to meet for coffee. They want to tell me about their life and what is going on. I love it!

Find one mentor and just stay focused on what you can focus on. Ignore the noise. And just move forward. Do your best every day. If you go in and do your best every day, you are going to be fine. Doing your best includes being prepared every day, doing your research, doing what you need to do to have a great class with the students.

But no, I am going to give them a big hug and tell them welcome. And then I would tell them to take it one step at a time.

Jonathan Alsheimer[29]

Middle School History Teacher, Author of "Next Level Teaching"

Do not try to be perfect! Be authentic. Try to make your lesson plans authentic and relevant. Try to understand what you are trying to teach your students and how this will be applicable to them.   Build relationships. Relationships and student engagement are the foundation of the work that we do.

You must set the tone as well. Have routines and consistency in your classroom and consistently build relationships with your students. Find ways to connect with them. Do not pick and choose who to connect

---

29. *Legendary Educator*, Episode 31

with or have favorites: every kid, every day, all year long. If they are unwilling to build that relationship with you, chip away at that ice until you get them at the end, even if it is the last week of school. But you are going to get them and you can tell them that I am coming at you every single day.

They cannot help but want to build a relationship with you because they walk into your classroom, and you have something cool for them. It might not be all class. You might have thirty minutes of the boring notes and this and that, but they know fifteen minutes of something cool is coming down the bridge and they cannot wait to come into that classroom. They cannot wait to go to math, language arts, and PE is finally fun because we are doing all this crazy stuff.

Bring it in there every single day. And just let your passion and your love for them show.

Michelle Ruhe[30]

Literacy Coach, Coach from the Couch

Do not compare yourself to your neighbor, especially if it is a veteran teacher. You do not come out of the gate as a veteran amazing teacher. I have been in education for twenty-three years and I am still not the teacher that I envisioned myself to be. It takes so much time. I have lots of room to grow and we all do.

---

30. *Legendary Educator,* Episode 16

Dr. Nairy Simon[31]

School Principal, New Generation International Schools

Do not be afraid! Teachers who have no idea about teaching and it is their first year will usually think that teaching is so cute from the movies they watch and the books they read, and they think when they enter the class, the kids really do sit down and they do listen. And that is not what happens inside the classroom. I am going to tell them do not be afraid of what you are going to see and what you are going to experience.

You have to come every day and get that out and you need to talk to somebody, whether your mentor or your coach, because it is frightening. It is scary when the teacher enters their classroom, especially new teachers who have never ever taught before, how their face glows and they have all those little stickers up there and the door is all shiny and pretty, and they have their markers set up. Then the kids come in and it is like something exploded in their face.

I have seen this happen before: teachers come out after their first session and they are like "Oh my God, what happened? Why are the kids acting this way? I didn't see that coming!" I would tell them not to be scared. It is going to be OK.

Teaching is not easy, especially now. Although teaching is one of the most rewarding jobs, it is the most challenging. But it is not impossible, it can be done, it just needs the right support system and the right group of people together so that you can make it happen.

----

31. *Legendary Educator,* Episode 12

Mark Evans[32]

Music Teacher (retired)

My advice is to know your limitations because you cannot do it all and you cannot know it all from the first day of school. Go in with your strengths and you will learn all those things that you need to along the way.

Do not be too hard on yourself and do not be too nervous around the kids. Act like you know what you are doing. Try to be as natural as possible. There are a lot of teachers that go into teaching and they just want to be very strict and show off their *teacher face* so the kids do not mess around. As a band teacher, I am in there with sixty kids with noise makers!

So my advice would just be to relax and take it easy. You do not have to know it all on the first day; just go into it and you will learn as you go. There are a lot of people out there that can help you as you go. Try to get a lot of continuing education as you go and talk to other teachers that are in your field.

And one of the best things I ever did was to travel around other schools when I was a young teacher to just watch other people teach and I learned a lot from that. So if you have that opportunity, I would say try to watch other teachers who have been at it for a while.

---

32. *Legendary Educator*, Episode 4

Naomi Hall[33]

Wellness Coach, The Recovering Educator

Take care of yourself! Make sure you are eating right. Make sure you are sleeping. Make sure you are managing stress outside of school. Remember that the behaviors and attitude you receive from your boss, your students, or parents are not about you – do not take it personally! Especially with the kids. There is much more to their behaviors than their reaction if I asked them to pick up a pencil and they lost it on me. I wish I had learned that a little sooner. Give the kids some grace. They blew up on you when you asked them to pick up the pencil. But, you know what? Something happened at home this morning. Something happened last class. Something else is going on with them. Try to give them a little grace and ask more questions rather than getting upset over the behavior; try to find out what is causing that behavior.

Steve Neal[34]

High School Teacher, Student Life Supervisor, St. Jude's Academy

Figure out what you are good at. Figure out what your strength is. Play to your strengths and get a good team around you because that is what gets you through.

I have this talk with our teachers each year during our August PD because at our school we use a House system, much like Harry Potter. I always take each of the teachers as a house off to the side and tell them "This

---

33. *Legendary Educator*, Episode 14

34. *Legendary Educator*, Episode 10

is your house. When it all falls apart, these are the teachers you go to. These are the ones that you get support from. They are here for you."

We do this whole yarn throwing game and it creates this huge web, which is the point. And then I have each of the teachers take a piece of the yarn off and tie it on their name tag and I tell them "Every time things are going bad in the classroom, look down and see that piece of yarn and remember, you are not alone. There is a web of us here." Get that team behind you because that is what gets you through.

Dr. Andrew Shipe[35]

High School English Literature Teacher, State Journalism Teacher of the Year, Pompano Beach High School

You were put in the classroom because someone has confidence in you. There will be times when you have a bad day. There will be times when you wonder if you are getting across to the kids. You will wonder if you are even up to it. Some days, it is just not a good day. It is not necessarily what happened, but a collection of what happened in you. You might ask yourself if you are doing the right thing, or if you are doing more harm than good.

After being a teacher for thirty years, even I have those feelings sometimes. Then I think about all my years of experience, and I have probably done more good than harm! I can look back on that and recognize that I am my biggest critic. You might have, what you believe, is a horrible day. But was it such a horrible day for your students? Maybe it was not all that horrible! So do not be unnecessarily hard on yourself.

---

35. Legendary Educator, Episode 3 & 33

This is actually a sign of a good teacher when you reflect back on your practices and think "What can I do better?" If a teacher like that comes to me and I see them being hard on themselves, that is how I know they are a good teacher, and they will improve because they are passionate and care about their job and about those kids.

Meet the Author

Ramez Takawy was born in Cairo, Egypt and was raised in Toronto, Canada; he holds both nationalities, identities, and personalities. He was an educator and instructional coach for over a decade until the global pandemic shut down schools worldwide; but he promises to return to the classroom soon!

In the meantime, Ramez hosts the *Legendary Educator* podcast, where he has inspirational conversations with experienced educators about successful teaching strategies. He also created *The Classroom Formula* professional development platform, starting with this book, then a sister podcast, and finally an intensive online course.

Ramez was naturally gifted in engaging his students, inspiring them to be curious and to learn, and has always displayed impeccable classroom management.

Connect with the Author

In-Person Professional Development

You can invite Ramez Takawy to come to your school to speak to your teachers or to lead in-person PD sessions. Ramez is always enthusiastic about talking to teachers and loves to travel around the world – no school is out of reach!

Speaking

Ramez is also available to speak at your education events and conferences.

To book Ramez for an in-person PD or a speaking engagement, please contact him at ramez@legendaryeducator.com

Follow on Social Media

Facebook – The Classroom Formula

Instagram - @theclassroomformula

YouTube - @legendaryeducator, @theclassroomformula

Additional Resources

A Gift for You!

I created a free gift just for you, as a token of my appreciation for reading my book! You can access it here: www.theclassroomformula.com/freegift

Podcast

The Classroom Formula is also available in an audio course format, so you can listen to it from wherever you are and whatever you are doing – also helpful if you are an auditory learner. You can access it here: www.theclassroomformula.com/podcast

Online Course

If you would like a more detailed and in-depth experience, *The Classroom Formula* online course is perfect for you. I take the points discussed in the book and discuss further, give more examples, and add more strategies and concepts that were not included in the book. You can access the online course here: www.theclassroomformula.com/course

Legendary Educator Podcast

If you would like to listen to my conversations with experienced educators, you can access the *Legendary Educator* podcast here: www. legendaryeducator.com/podcast

legendaryeducator.com/podcast

Contributors

Michelle Ruhe
coachfromthecouch.com

Michelle Ruhe is a 25-year veteran educator, currently serving as a K-5 literacy coach. Michelle works alongside teachers in classrooms every day, and fully understands the challenges today's teachers face. It is her mission to help as many educators as she can to streamline, simplify, and strengthen their classroom instruction through her online coaching service.

Alissa Crabtree

crabtreecoachingcollaborative.org

Alissa Crabtree, a dedicated educator with over 17 years of experience, has made an indelible mark in the field of education. As a seasoned writer and instructional leadership coach, she brings a unique perspective to her work. At the helm of Crabtree Coaching Collaborative LLC, Alissa collaborates with campus and district leaders, alleviating educator overwhelm by strategically aligning vision and enhancing collective efficacy.

Crabtree Coaching Collaborative provides hands-on and continuous support that you will not find with larger companies. Her mission is to rescue instructional leaders from overwhelm, turning their teams into impact superheroes (no capes required!).

So, when you are ready to transform your campus, call Alissa, and let's accelerate your impact!

Dr. Naomi Hall

<u>therecoveringeducator.com</u>

Dr. Naomi Hall is a veteran educator with 20 years of experience ranging from classroom teacher to district administrator to consultant. She has personally experienced burnout and extreme stress. She uses practical steps to help professionals build effective stress management habits and make a comeback from burnout. Her goal is to help stressed out and overwhelmed professionals take back control of their lives. You can come back from stress and burnout, and she knows how to do it.

Dr. Hall supports her clients through her stress management coaching and as a partner with BODi, the health and wellness company. She helps her clients build a solid foundation of stress management through healthy habit formation.

Professionals hire Naomi to help them gain control of their lives so they can love their life and career again.

Miriam Burlakovsky
MindfulMiri.com

Miriam Burlakovsky is known for her mindful mental health solutions. With a terminal degree in psychology and extensive training in mindfulness, she has established herself as an expert in school-based mental and behavioral health. She is a Licensed Educational Psychologist (#4368), Board Certified Behavior Analyst (BCBA), Mindfulness Teacher, and Yoga Teacher (RYT) with over 17 years in education.

About Defining Moments Press

Built for aspiring authors who are looking to share transformative ideas with others throughout the world, Defining Moments Press offers life coaches, healers, business professionals, and other non-fiction or self-help authors a comprehensive solution to getting their books published without breaking the bank or taking years. Defining Moments Press prides itself on bringing readers and authors together to find tools and solutions.

As an alternative to self-publishing or signing with a major publishing house, we offer full profits to our authors, low-priced author copies, and simple contract terms.

Most authors get stuck trying to navigate the technical end of publishing. The comprehensive publishing services offered by Defining Moments Press mean that your book will be designed by an experienced graphic artist, available in printed, hard copy format, and coded for all eBook readers, including the Kindle, iPad, Nook, and more.

We handle all the technical aspects of your book creation so you can spend more time focusing on your business that makes a difference for other people.

Defining Moments Press founder, publisher, and #1 bestselling author Melanie Warner has over 20 years of experience as a writer, publisher, master life coach, and accomplished entrepreneur.

You can learn more about Warner's innovative approach to self-publishing or take advantage of free training and education at: MyDefiningMoments.com.

DEFINING MOMENTS BOOK PUBLISHING

If you're like many authors, you have wanted to write a book for a long time, maybe you have even started a book ... but somehow, as hard as you have tried to make your book a priority, other things keep getting in the way.

Some authors have fears about their ability to write or whether anyone will value what they write or buy their book. For others, the challenge is making the time to write their book or having accountability to finish it.

It's not just finding the time and confidence to write that is an obstacle. Most authors get overwhelmed with the logistics of finding an editor, finding a support team, hiring an experienced designer, and figuring out all the technicalities of writing, publishing, marketing, and launching a book. Others have written a book and might have even published it but did not find a way to make it profitable.

For more information on how to participate in our next Defining Moments Author Training program, visit www.MyDefiningMoments.com

Or

email support@MyDefiningMoments.com

OTHER #1 BESTSELLING BOOKS BY DEFINING MOMENTS ™ PRESS

Defining Moments: Coping With the Loss of a Child—Melanie Warner

Defining Moments SOS: Stories of Survival—Melanie Warner and Amber Torres

Write your Bestselling Book in 8 Weeks or Less and Make a Profit—Even if No One Has Ever Heard of You—Melanie Warner

Become Brilliant: Roadmap From Fear to Courage—Shiran Cohen

Unspoken: Body Language and Human Behavior For Business—Shiran Cohen

Rise, Fight, Love, Repeat: Ignite Your Morning Fire—Jeff Wickersham

Life Mapping: Decoding the Blueprint of Your Soul—Karen Loenser

Ravens and Rainbows: A Mother-Daughter Story of Grit, Courage and Love After Death—L. Grey and Vanessa Lynn

Pivot You! 6 Powerful Steps to Thriving During Uncertain Times—Suzanne R. Sibilla

A Workforce Inspired: Tools to Manage Negativity and Support a Toxic-Free Workplace—Dolores Neira

Journey of 1000 Miles: A Musher and His Huskies' Journey on the Century-Old Klondike Trails—Hank DeBruin and Tanya McCready

7 Unstoppable Starting Powers: Powerful Strategies for Unparalleled Results From Your First Year as a New Leader—Olusegun Eleboda

Bouncing Back From Divorce With Vitality & Purpose: A Strategy For Dads—Nigel J. Smart, PhD

Focus on Jesus and Not the Storm: God's Non-negotiables to Christians in America—Keith Kelley

Stepping Out, Moving Forward: Songs and Devotions—Jacqueline O'Neil Kelley

Time Out for Time In: How Reconnecting With Yourself Can Help You Bond With Your Child in a Busy Word—Jerry Le

The Sacred Art of Off Mat Yoga: Whisper of Wisdom Forever—Shakti Barnhill

The Beauty of Change: The Fun Way for Women to Turn Pain Into Power & Purpose—Jean Amor Ramoran

From No Time to Free Time: 6 Steps to Work/Life Balance for Business Owners—Christoph Nauer

Self-Healing for Sexual Abuse Survivors: Tired of Just Surviving, Time to Thrive—Nickie V. Smith

Prepared Bible Study Lessons: Weekly Plans for Church Leaders—John W. Warner

Frog on a Lily Pad—Michael Lehre

How to Effectively Supercharge Your Career as a CEO—Giorgio Pasqualin

Rising From Unsustainable: Replacing Automobiles and Rockets—J.P. Sweeney

Food—Life's Gift for Healing: Simple, Delicious & Life Saving Whole Food Plant Based Solutions—Angel and Terry Grier

Harmonize All of You With All: The Leap Ahead in Self-Development—Artie Vipperla

Powerless to Powerful: How to Stop Living in Fear and Start Living Your Life—Kat Spencer

Living with Dirty Glasses: How to Clean those Dirty Glasses and Gain a Clearer Perspective Of Your Life—Leah Montani

The Road Back to You: Finding Your Way After Losing a Child to Suicide—Trish Simonson

Gavin Gone: Turning Pain into Purpose to Create a Legacy—Rita Gladding

The Health Nexus: TMJ, Sleep Apnea, and Facial Development, Causations and Treatment—Robert Perkins DDS

Samantha Jean's Rainbow Dream: A Young Foster Girl's Adventure into the Colorful World of Fruits & Vegetables—AJ Autieri-Luciano

Live Your Truth: An Arab Man's Journey In Finding the Courage to Live His Truth As He Identifies as Gay and Coping with Mental Illness—David Rabadi

Unstoppable: A Parent's Survival Guide for Special Education Services with an IEP or 504 Plan—Raja B. Marhaba

Please, Excuse My Brave: Overcoming Fear and Living Out Your Purpose—Anisa Wesley

Drawing with Purpose: A Sketch Journal—Rick Alonzo

NY Coffee: Love Fulfilled in the Little Things—Craig Lieckfelt

Good Work: How Gen X and Millennials are the Dream Team for Doing Good When Collaborating—Erin Kate Whitcomb

Rescue Me: Guided Self-Healing for First Responders: Conquering Depression, Anxiety, PTSD & Moral Injury—David Hogan

Treasures In Grief: Discover 7 Spiritual Gifts Hidden in Your Pain—Lo Anne Mayer

We Three: Their Beginnings—Derek Drummond

Ripping off the Mask—Joseph Lee

Culture Spin—Kristy Wachter

Discover Your Inner Leader—Mamta Goyal

Grit, Growth and Gumption for Women: Three Keys To Lead Yourself and Others With Confidence—Tinsley English